Rats

Bats and

Strange

Toilets

Travel Tips for Unusual Countries

David Freemantle

A Zymurgy Publishing book

First published in Great Britain by
Zymurgy Publishing in 2006

Cover design Nick Ridley

A CIP catalogue record for this book is available from the British
Library.

Printed and bound by Bookmarque, U.K.

10 9 8 7 6 5 4 3 2 1

ISBN 1 903506 21 2
ISBN 9781903506219
Zymurgy Publishing
Newcastle upon Tyne

Dedication

To love a country is to love its people. Without exception in each of the fifty or more countries I have visited I have encountered special people.

I dedicate this book to just two very special people who live in an unusual country. I have come to know them well:

ILENE GUILLENO and her sister AGNES

Both are glowing examples of the ancient adage that even in material poverty and with little formal education you can be rich in spirit. Both epitomize goodness and are for me an inspiration.

Acknowledgement

In hindsight I have been negligent. I failed to note the names of all the wonderful people I've met around the world who contributed in some small way to the material in this book. My excuse is that many of the travel experiences upon which I draw took place before the idea of writing the book occurred to me.

I am grateful to Michael Freemantle for the initial stimulus. Over a leisurely meal one evening I told him about the cockroaches I had encountered in my hotel room on a recent trip. Being a twin brother he immediately trumped my story by telling me about the rat he had discovered in a foreign hotel room. Driving home that night the idea for the book occurred to me. It is often the little incidents that colour our experiences of travel.

Years later with the book near completion I shared some of the material with three people from unusual countries and I am grateful for their helpful comments. These are Stephanie Fock Dick Wing whom I've known a fair while and two recent acquaintances Jessica Deutsch and Mhay Regalario.

However I am most indebted to a rather unusual person. He is Martin Ellis my publisher and editor. Rather unusually he decided to publish my book. Having agreed a time-table I eventually submitted to him what I thought was the perfect book. He immediately found its imperfections. We had quite a few disagreements as I attempted to defend my imperfections. However Martin normally won the argument. The end result is a far better book than I had originally written. I am most grateful for that. Thank you Martin. Thank you Michael, Stephanie, Jessica and Mhay and many others who have contributed.

Author details

David Freemantle is the author of 14 business books and is based in Windsor, UK.

He was born in Southampton and now works presenting business seminars around the world having previously been on the board of an airline.

During his career he has travelled extensively (to over 50 different countries) and this book is based on his experiences.

His globe-trotting to and around unusual countries continues.

To find out more about David Freemantle, visit his web site www.superboss.co.uk

Contents

Chapter 7 199

Strange Experiences: Things To See And Avoid In Unusual Countries

Chapter 8   225

In Preparation For Travel To Unusual Countries: The Final Lists

INTRODUCTION

You've not arrived until you've been to the toilet. Then you can apply your mind to the real purpose of your journey. A friend once told me "The first thing I think about when travelling are the toilets." Whether you are visiting the local shopping mall or a far-flung corner of the world, toilets will be uppermost on your mind.

There are two types of toilets. The first type are ones we have back home which we are used to. These are the usual toilets you find in what I designate as 'usual' countries. However, there are other countries where the toilets can be rather strange, at least outside the confines of your hotel – and sometimes inside. These countries are what I designate as 'unusual'. It is not only strange toilets that qualify countries as being 'unusual' but hundreds of other memorable features such as the rats you may occasionally find in your hotel room or the bats that enter your open window and fly around above your bed in the middle of the night.

This book therefore is about the unusual experiences you are going to have when travelling to 'unusual' countries, whether you be a backpacker, a rather adventurous tourist, visiting a friend, a foreign student, a charity worker, an embassy official, a computer expert or a business person. To help with your stay in the 'unusual' country this book also offers you a wide range of practical tips on how to deal with the strange situations you will inevitably find yourself in.

For normal travel from one 'usual' country to another a key issue is 'convergence'. A tourist experience in one country can converge into an almost identical experience in another country. For example, as a tourist you might be visiting the Mall at Cribbs Causeway where you can sit, relax and sip your caffe latte in a rather nice indoor piazza with sunlight streaming down on you and pleasant indoor plants beautifying your surrounds. A few steps away is the usual Burger King and around the corner is a Crabtree & Evelyn, a Virgin Megastore, a Sony Centre, a Sunglasses Hut, Monsoon, Millie's Cookies,

KFC, Pizza Hut, Nandos, Starbucks Coffee and countless other stores you can see in most 'usual' countries. And of course I forgot to mention the Disney Store.

Outside is a vast car park (with 10,000 places) beyond which is your favourite T.G.I.Friday's, a massive supermarket, a bowling alley, a cinema complex and just a little further away a hotel. You could be in the USA, Europe, South Africa, the Middle East, the Far East or somewhere else.

You would in fact be in Bristol, England, although you would be forgiven for thinking that you were in Sawgrass Mills Florida, or the Seef Shopping Mall Bahrain, or the Tyger Vallei Mall Cape Town, or in Petronas Towers Kuala Lumpur, or the Rockwell Center Metro Manila or that vast retail complex at Calais, France, near the entrance to the Channel Tunnel or one of those modern shopping malls like SunTec in Singapore (where the only pastime is shopping).

As shopping malls around the world become all the same, the danger is that as individuals, we become all the same too. As global citizens we only have three ways of communicating with each other nowadays and that's by having cellphones stuck permanently to our ears or by using email or SMS text messaging. Old fashioned social interaction is slowly becoming obsolete, there is no need when you have hi-tech.

The films in cinemas are all the same and the television is all the same. Every hotel in the world seems to have CNN.

And that brings me to another subject. All the modern hotels in the world are the same. Once you have been to one Novotel you have been to them all. Every bedroom is identical. The same applies to most large hotel chains, the same old breakfasts, the same old club sandwiches, the same expensive colas and the same long queues and indifferent service.

When not in hotels many people often eat the same fast food (burgers, fries and pizzas) and drink the same colas and caffe lattes.

As we hop around the world from one tourist attraction to another it is rare to encounter an individual who doesn't speak English, doesn't wear jeans and T-shirts and who doesn't listen to English rock music or American rap.

We encapsulate our boredom by fixing cameras to our eyes and taking millions of photos and video sequences which no one ever looks at.

However, it is not for me to be a prophet of doom. There is hope yet. There is still time to protect our environment, our atmosphere and the real world as we used to know it before the monotonous repetitiveness of global capitalism in our 'usual' countries anaesthetises us with massive doses of milk and honey and kills us off with acute hypoglycaemia and related modern diseases.

The real world still does exist if you look for it and you are prepared to ease yourself away from shopping malls, forego your cellphone and laptop then venture out. Beyond the confines of your usual comfort zones are countries that are guaranteed to excite should you be prepared to take a risk or two. These are countries where the nearest Starbucks and MacDonalds is a thousand miles away. There are unusual delicacies in local restaurants waiting to be discovered.

With the creeping Americanisation of the world these 'unusual' countries are becoming increasingly rare. However, there is still time enough to visit them. There you will find things a little bit different from what you are used to. You will have innumerable unusual experiences and a more than adequate supply of fascinating stories to take back home and bore your friends and relations with (in the piazza in the shopping mall).

This book is all about the unusual experiences you might expect in 'unusual' countries and aims to provide you with a series of useful insights, advice and tips on how to deal with these experiences – for example, rats and bats in your hotel bedroom and encounters with strange toilets.

In writing this book I have drawn on in-depth research I have undertaken during the last twenty years in visiting over fifty 'unusual' countries. (I couldn't sleep the other night and counted them). I have taken care not to identify any of them as I didn't want to offend any one I might accidentally leave out.

As soon as you read the first section you will realise the seriousness of the issues presented here. I apologise for this. However, travelling in this 'unusual' world should be fun and therefore I have tried to lighten your load with a little levity.

CHAPTER 1

ANIMALS IN UNUSUAL COUNTRIES

There are only three types of animals: pets, pests and protein-generators. Few pets exist in unusual countries. It is the pests that are dominant and they only have one law: "survival of the fittest". They have no particular interest in protecting or romanticising human beings who, in the main, they see as predators. If their brains were big enough these pests would die of heart attacks if they learnt that we human beings go out of our way to protect them. This goes against all the laws of nature.

In this chapter you will be introduced to some of the animals that you are most likely to encounter whilst travelling in unusual countries. The only interest they have in you is to exploit you if not eat you. At best they want to be left alone so that they can get on and kill other animals or destroy the environment.

As many of these species cannot even protect themselves against predation and extinction let alone protect the planet which feeds them — it is left to us eccentric soft-hearted but war mongering humans to do so. We are not doing a good job at the moment.

I RATS

Rats can be a problem in hotel rooms despite the internet, email, SMS text messages, global telecommunications and other wonderful advances in modern technology (not forgetting, of course, Google).

When you have a rat in your room you will hear a scraping sound approximately fifteen minutes after going to bed and just as you are about to doze off.

When you turn the light on you will see nothing and you will wonder whether it was a bad dream. You will turn the light off and fifteen minutes later the scraping sound will start again.

The thing to do is to lie perfectly still and allow your eyes to acclimatise to the darkness. Should there be sufficient moonlight you might be lucky enough to see a dark rat-like object (which is in fact a rat) poking its nose around the floor of your bedroom. Rats are intelligent creatures and know that housekeeping in hotels is not that efficient. It will know that before retiring you will snack on the oat cookie you sneaked from the aeroplane. Furthermore, it will know that you will drop crumbs onto the floor which housekeeping will fail to sweep up. (The key thing is not to leave cookie crumbs on your lips, chin, face, pillow or sheet).

It is pointless trying to hit the rat with a rolled-up newspaper because as soon as you move the rat will disappear. Laying down rat poison does work after a few days but has the disadvantage of producing dead rats that you will have to remove personally. You will also need to take rat poison with you.

My brother Mike told me that when he discovered a rat in his hotel room he informed reception. They offered to send up a cat. If you are made this offer do not take it up. Cats in in unusual countries are more lethal than rats (see section on CATS AND DOGS).

There is an easy solution to the rat problem, which Mike discovered. He tested it and it always works. I use it all the time now. Turn on your television and keep the sound low. Rats are frightened of televisions and will not enter the room when one is on, especially if it is CNN (with all those disaster scenes and pictures of wailing people).

Keeping the television on also has the added advantage that it will send you to sleep (which invariably happens when I watch it at home after the evening meal).

Tip For Your Trip

Take a small portable television with you (in case there's no TV in your room).

2 BATS

Twice recently I have been awoken by a flapping sound in my hotel bedroom.

On both occasions there had been a power cut (see section on POWER FAILURES) and the air-conditioning was not working. Before going to bed I had therefore opened the window to let some air in.

The next thing I knew was that I had a bat circling my room in a mad panic. When you have just been dreaming of better things, to be awoken to the sight of jagged black wings skittering around above your head in the moonlight can be rather frightening.

There are three options for removing flying bats from your room, each to be tried progressively if the previous option fails.

OPTION ONE

Do nothing. The bat has very sensitive, sonic orientation and will be bouncing its sound signals off the walls trying to work out how to escape. Try this for ten minutes. If this fails try Option Two.

OPTION TWO

Talk to the bat in a low (baritone) voice. This might be difficult if you are female. However, if you speak slowly and repeat the words "please leave the room" (preferably in English) it will eventually get the message and leave. It is more frightened of your voice than you. Sometimes local languages also work. If this fails try Option Three.

OPTION THREE

This is the most drastic option. Stand naked in the middle of the bed and flap a towel at the bat. It will circle the room even faster and become more frightened — not of your nakedness but of your flapping towel. After ten minutes it will flop in a corner totally exhausted, drained of all energy and unable to fly. At this point take the cardboard box you have been carrying with you and scoop the bat (using a copy of this book opened at this page) into the box. Leave the box on the ledge outside the window. In the morning the bat will be gone.

Tip For Your Trip

Never open your window at night when sleeping in unusual countries. Most bats are blind if not bonkers. They can't even fly straight. Always take a cardboard box with you.

3 COCKROACHES

Cockroaches are not difficult to recognise. If you visit your hotel bathroom in the middle of the night and see a large insect about an inch long scurrying away across the tiles into some dark hole it is definitely a cockroach. It will have a black or brown oval body, threadlike antennae and look positively evil. This is because it will be up to no good at all.

Some cockroaches have wings and will fly through your window just to get a drink. They love those little globules of water you carelessly spray around. So make sure you dry your face properly before going to sleep.

If you try to hit a cockroach with a copy of this book it will just laugh before scooting off.

If you complain to the hotel management they will also laugh at you and tell you it was only yesterday that they fumigated the room - no wonder there are cockroaches all over the place, they have been flushed out!

Some people have tried taking a hammer with them to kill these horrible creatures but this tends to destroy the bathroom tiling rather than cockroaches. However, there is an effective tool that is guaranteed to work. This is a lady's high heel shoe (it is immaterial whether it is a left or right footed shoe).

These shoes have excellent aerodynamics, flexible movement and cause little damage to bathroom surrounds whilst inflicting certain fatality on an offending cockroach. Creep up on the creature stealthily with the shoe poised above your shoulder and then with a fast flick of the wrist flatten the cockroach with the heel of the shoe.

Female guests in hotels will have no problem with the above solution.

Sadly to say, male shoes are much less effective with greatly reduced accuracy and flattening power. Unaccompanied male readers should therefore endeavour to take a lady's high heel shoe with them on their travels. Should they forget, then it is suggested they venture down to the hotel bar, approach a lady with high heel shoes and offer her a complimentary share of a bed for the night (together with a free breakfast) in exchange for the use of one of her shoes, should that be necessary.

Tip For Your Trip

Pack a lady's high heel shoe (it doesn't have to be the latest fashion model).

4 MOSQUITOES

Whilst rats, bats and cockroaches are quite visible and easy to chase off, mosquitoes are difficult to entrap and kill.

The flies in colder climes tend to be slow and not very streetwise, they appear in your room in daylight, make a lot of noise and then quickly surrender by the window virtually begging for you to exterminate them with a rolled-up newspaper. In fact, English flies are well known for high stress levels and a suicidal tendency.

By comparison, mosquitoes in unusual countries are well trained terrorists. They work at night, carry malaria and are determined to infect you.

They normally buzz you just as you are trying to get to sleep. You can try pulling the sheet over your head but they will still get at you. Close to your exposed ear you will hear a sporadic whirring noise as the mosquito circles the room and practices dive bombing your head.

If you turn on the light they make themselves virtually invisible, you might just catch an occasional glimpse of one in a shaft of light. No matter how hard you look you will never see this mosquito resting on a window pane or dancing around a light bulb, it is far too clever remaining out of eyesight and earshot until you turn off the light again.

Here is what to do. There are two options.

OPTION ONE
Fill your room with smoke. (Cuban cigars are recommended). This will drive away the mosquito. Please note that there are substantial immediate fire risks with this option and substantial long term health risks too. In some countries this can also be politically incorrect.

OPTION TWO
Ask your partner to cut a fresh onion into two and then to rub your naked body from top to toe with its malodorous flesh (you can practice on your partner first). This will deter mosquitoes from descending upon you as they cannot stand the smell of onions.

In certain unusual countries this technique is used as a form of contraception.

Tip For Your Trip

On arriving at your mosquito infested hotel purchase six Cuban cigars, a box of matches and a fresh juicy onion. If these are not available ensure you pack these items before departing. Then invite someone with whom you desire to be intimate to cut the onion in half and rub its flesh into your naked body. It is imperative that you then reciprocate.

5 CATS AND DOGS

In the real world cats and dogs are nothing like those charming pets that appear in television advertisements or those animals that make a mess on your own kitchen floor.

For a start, in unusual countries cats and dogs are rarely allowed inside houses, so they have to roam the streets scavenging for food. The only animals that are allowed inside houses are chickens, goats and sheep.

Cats and dogs are not considered as pets in these unusual countries. Their existence is purely functional. Cats are there to keep mice and rats away whilst dogs are meant to chase off strangers. Neither do a very good job.

They scrape a living off the street, putting a nose into everything and collecting a skin full of fleas en route. They wander around aimlessly investigating anything sufficiently revolting to be of interest. Most of these cats and dogs are scraggy, underfed, have sores on their backs and look as if they haven't had a wash for many months.

Nobody owns these cats and dogs and they tend to do their breeding whenever they want (much like us humans). They have a tendency to fight in the middle of the night and make a lot a noise, in fact there are dogs in unusual countries that can bark all night long without anybody strangling them.

Much as you might love cats and dogs in your own country it is unwise to befriend one of these animals during a visit to an unusual country, no matter how appealingly they look at you.

Should you be foolish enough to step outside your hotel and give one of these animals a scrap of food it will follow you around for the rest of your trip.

The more adventurous cats and dogs will gravitate towards open air restaurants where they will try to rub their lousy backs against your leg or jump onto your table when you are trying to eat. If they pester you it is best to hit them with a stick (an old fashioned headmaster's cane is best for this). Alternatively you can poke them in their eyes with chopsticks.

Tip For Your Trip

Always carry an old fashioned headmaster's cane and/or a pair of cheap chopsticks.

6 LIONS

Those of you who have read the previous five sections of this book will realise that it is not advisable to leave the window of your bedroom open at night. However, if you do there is another risk when visiting unusual countries.

We were advised of this one evening by a local guide who had spent the day helping us search for lion dung. As we sat around the camp fire at our exotic mosquito infested retreat in the bush he asked:

"What would you do if you woke up tonight and found a lion staring at you through the open window?"

"Panic." said one young woman.

"Take a photograph!" I retorted promptly.

However, the guide, who posed the question knew from experience what the correct answer was.

"You have to pretend to be dead." he told us "Lions never eat meat that's been lying around dead for a few days. They like their meat really fresh. Therefore, my advice is to always wear stinking dirty old clothes in bed and remain dead still if you encounter a lion. Even if it's curious enough to come and paw you, still don't move. It will then get bored and move away."

He then went on to inform us that for a lion to attack a human being it has to meet at least three of the following five criteria:

(a) It will have red eyes

(b) It will be female (male lions are much too lazy to do any work and leave all the hunting to females)

(c) It will be mad (not angry mad but insane mad)

(d) It will be very very hungry

(e) Fed up with wildebeest it will be looking for a new diet

Tip For Your Trip

Ensure you wear dirty, stinking clothes (this can save on laundry bills too).

7 TIGERS

Tigers not only look different from lions but they actually like eating human beings. In fact, a human being is to a tiger what a crispy aromatic duck is to a human being.

Tigers are also very determined. When they spot a juicy specimen of human being they will often trail the person for two or three days before choosing the perfect moment to attack.

It is little known that tigers are excellent swimmers and often follow their prey (for example, inshore fishermen) into water to capture them. Tigers can swim faster than most other mammals.

Walking or swimming around in a wire cage to prevent attack from tigers is not a viable option.

The more sensible thing to do is not go walking if you suspect there are tigers in the locality.

However, if you insist there is a well-tried technique which is guaranteed to work on fifty-one per cent of occasions.

Apparently, according to experts, tigers are stealthy and only attack from behind. Unlike lions they will never charge you from the front. So you will not know you are being attacked by a tiger until it has your neck in its jaws.

To prevent attack you should wear a face-mask on the back of your head. This face-mask should be as lifelike as possible. You can even pull a few strings if you want to be sophisticated. The tiger will think it is facing you and not attack.

Tip For Your Trip

Purchase a lifelike face-mask at a local souvenir shop in an unusual country, then when out in the countryside wear it on the back of your head.

8 CROCODILES

This is not the place to go into a lengthy debate about the difference between a crocodile and an alligator. Anyone who has been on the brink of being eaten alive by either of these animals will know how ugly they are and the irrelevance of identifying the species.

On very hot days be very wary of going swimming let alone paddling in that attractive lake or river that you have just come across.

In all likelihood there is a crocodile lurking just beneath the water's surface. The crocodile can stay under water for a very long time before briefly pushing its snout to the surface for air. At this point you will think it is just a log floating in this dreamy creek.

As soon as you step into the water you are as good as gone. Quick as a flash the crocodile will grab your ankle and drag you into the water. Do not worry, it will not start eating you there and then. In fact, it will allow you a more humane death by drowning you first. This is its game plan. It will keep you under water until you are dead. Then it will take its time to devour you. The digestion tract of a crocodile works very slowly and it can take up to three months for the flesh of a large mammal to work its way through the crocodile's system. Therefore the crocodile is in no mad rush to chew you to bits. Crocodiles tend not to eat every day but enjoy one large meal every few weeks. They consider human beings to be a particularly rare delicacy.

If you insist on paddling barefoot and believe crocodiles might be around you can test the water by throwing into it a live chicken or a large piece of fresh fillet steak. If a reptilian tail flashes and the steak is gone in a split second you will know there is a crocodile in the water.

Tip For Your Trip

Before approaching a lake, river or creek visit a local butcher and purchase some best fillet steak. If this is not available ask him to sell you a live chicken (it's going to die anyway). The final option is to capture a stray cat and throw it in the creek to test for crocodiles. It is advisable not to use rats for this purpose.

9 PIRANHAS

Our guide was holding court on the veranda of a resting lodge on the edge of a rain forest. Just down the muddy path was a piranha infested river. Naturally the conversation turned to piranhas.

The guide, who was arrogant and claimed to know everything, told us that piranhas were much maligned and had suffered from much adverse publicity about their predatory flesh-eating habits.

He asserted that it was a myth that when piranhas scented blood they would attack a mammal, tear it apart with their sharp teeth and consume it in an instant. He asserted there was no recorded incident of this ever happening to a man (let alone a woman). What he did tell us was that piranhas did occasionally nip the bodies of other fish and even their fellow brethren. This was because piranhas were attracted to the oil in their skins. (Fish oils are not only good for human beings but also for fish).

He volunteered to prove his theory. He went to his room, changed and returned in an old-fashioned swimming costume. Pulling out a safety razor he slid it roughly over his right cheek, causing a few globules of blood to trickle down to his chin.

He then wandered nonchalantly down to where a canoe was moored to the creaking wooden jetty and dived into the gently flowing tropical river. We watched him swim around the bend and out of sight towards the pygmy camp in the jungle half-a-mile away. This caused much conversation. The wide-eyed monkeys squawked too and clambered up the trees opposite.

We stayed up to midnight waiting for him to return but by this time we were all so tired we went to bed. He didn't even join us for breakfast the next morning. A couple of days after his disappearance we donated his clothes to the pygmies and then, with their help, trekked back through the rain forest to the airstrip and waited for our biplane.

We often wondered what happened to our guide. However, we were confident that whatever he did he knew what he was doing. Personally, I thought he was a little irresponsible to leave us stranded in the rain forest. After all, he had even mentioned that the previous generation of pygmies in the camp nearby had been cannibals. But now they all had cellphones, diesel generators and television sets. One even had a refrigerator.

The ageing pygmy chief did not join us on our trek back through the rain forest. Apparently he had stomach problems and was being tended to by his thirty wives.

Tip For Your Trip

If your tour guide lacks common sense use your own.

10 ELEPHANTS

Normally these huge animals are not dangerous except in rare circumstances.

First a word of warning: left to their own devices elephants will destroy the planet. These lucky creatures have been romanticised as famous cartoon characters, are heroes in films and are protected by crazed environmentalists.

In reality elephants are as bad if not worse than rats. I have seen a family of elephants in the bush tearing down tree after tree. If left unchecked they would clear the rain forests at a faster rate than a bulldozer.

Elephants eat everything that is green on a tree. They destroy trees and can ravage a whole forest. They are the most environmentally unfriendly animals on earth.

However, elephants look nice and are good for photographs. Therefore, we must protect them.

Elephants prefer to be left to their own devices, in which case they will leave you to your own. They will not disturb you unless you disturb them.

The most disturbing thing for any of these animals is when you come between them and their offspring. Should you unwisely separate a mother from her young then she is guaranteed to trample you underfoot. Remember, these animals weigh tons. Whilst not wanting to eat you they will leave you as pulp if you dare step between them and their kids.

Tip For Your Trip

Never separate an elephant from its offspring. Just in case always wear an armour-plated metal waistcoat and jockstrap in the vicinity of elephants.

11 GORILLAS

Gorillas are curious creatures. They are a bit like human beings really, being very curious about people they meet in everyday life.

Whilst most wild animals will run a mile to avoid a human being a gorilla will do the reverse. A gorilla will be absolutely fascinated when he (or she - they are very sensitive to political correctness) comes across a human being.

The first thing a gorilla will want to do is make friends and show you his (or her) love and affection. He will do this by bounding up to you, raking his hand through your hair and trying to tear off your clothes. Do not be alarmed by this, it really is a sign of friendship. Furthermore you might think, whilst the gorilla has you in its clutches, that it is trying to bite off your nose and ear, but actually it is the gorilla's way of kissing. The human touch and cuddling are very important to a gorilla.

However, there is one thing you must never do with a gorilla and this has been proved by students of gorilla psychology. And that is look a gorilla in the eyes. When you stare a gorilla in the eyes he will see this as a threat and therefore you as an enemy. In many parts of the world eye contact is definitely not on and causes offence.

Should you inadvertently glance at a gorilla's eyes do not even attempt to apologise. He will not understand. Instead he will want to kill you, immediately.

The best form of protection against being killed by gorillas is to wear dark sunglasses. The gorilla might try to remove them from you but whilst studying and playing with them you will have a great opportunity to escape. However do not pause to take photographs as this is akin to looking a gorilla in the eyes. Unless of course the gorilla is already wearing your sunglasses in which case there will be no problem.

Tip For Your Trip

Always wear dark gorilla-proof sunglasses in the vicinity of gorillas.

12 MONKEYS AND MINAH BIRDS

There are some really clever people around. They train animals, not to perform for entertainment but to steal.

On one occasion I was being driven to a local beauty spot on the top of a mountain in an unusual country. We came to a lay-by with a really wonderful panoramic view of the jungle below and the craggy mountains above. I asked the driver to pull up.

In the lay-by were the usual stall-holders selling T-shirts and postcards as well as practicing their English. There was also a hawker selling infectious icecream from a rusting metal container and another offering stale prawns in pancakes.

I didn't see the other guy and his monkey. I went to take a photograph and suddenly I felt a movement on my shoulder and then sensed the cash I had in the upper left hand breast pocket of my shirt had gone missing.

I spotted a man running down the road with a monkey on his shoulder. The monkey was still grasping my money. Fortunately my driver had seen this and had reversed the car on this dangerous hairpin bend and chased after the thief.

He caught up, the man stopped. I could see a heated argument taking place.

The monkey eventually handed back the money and the driver returned it. I was so grateful I gave the driver ten dollars as a tip for his valiant efforts.

It was only later I realised what the racket was. My driver was in league with the thief and the monkey. They played out this act on every trip. Of the ten dollars 'reward' the thief would later get half.

A friend told me there is another racket in this country by which thieves train up minah birds to fly into the hotel rooms of people who foolishly leave their windows a fraction ajar (didn't I warn you earlier about leaving your windows open?). These small birds squeeze through the smallest of openings and then do a thorough search of the hotel bedrooms searching for bright items such as diamond rings and gold jewellery.

You must admit it that there are some clever thieves in this world. How can you send a minah bird or monkey to prison?

Tip For Your Trip

Never expose your cash to monkeys or diamond rings to minah birds.

13 BABOONS

Human beings do not rule the world. Baboons do. To be exact it is the alpha male of the species who is in charge. The rest of the group just stand and watch when he confronts an innocent human.

The alpha baboon will boss the family around as they scavenge amongst litter bins in car parks – taking full advantage of us lower orders in the genealogy who squander huge portions of French fries and crispy chickens for the benefit of baboons.

Do not expose anything to these animals. They will grab cheeseburgers, cola cans, camcorders as well as drag carrier bags off you to share the contents with their family and friends. They will not take 'no' for an answer, will not be frightened off and will scoff and then growl if you try to beat them away.

These animals bare their ugly pink bums, are totally lacking in sexual decorum and are more raucous than British MPs at parliamentary 'Question Time'. Baboons are real 'toughies'. Soccer hooligans use them as role models.

Tip For Your Trip

Never urinate in the presence of baboons.

Also avoid eating anything when they are around.

When you see a pack of baboons roaming through your neighbourhood or swinging through the trees, then you should get into your car and drive away like a real coward.

14 EAGLES

One of the world's largest eagles is the Crowned Eagle. It has been known to swoop down on a sweet baby antelope and carry it away with its claws. It has claws on its elbows as well as its feet.

Normally a Crowned Eagle is satisfied with eating large juicy monkeys. However, sometimes it mistakes human beings for monkeys, especially small human beings.

So if you are out walking in an unusual forest, enjoying fresh air, sun and romantic jungle-like woodlands beware of eagles. You will not see them before they attack, as they will perch on the top of a tall tree and when your back is turned they will swoop down on you and carry you off to some perilous destination where you will be unable to escape whilst they make a meal of you, initially carrying bits of human (commonly known as carrion) back to their lovely little baby chicks high up in their nests beyond the reach of man.

This is what nature lovers love and is why throughout the world we go out of our way to protect eagles, not that eagles go out of their way to protect us.

There are a number of common sense strategies you can adopt to prevent eagle attack. The first is to wear a large wide-brimmed black hat. This will confuse the eagle so at worst you will lose your hat. The second is to wear a polystyrene cape over your neck and shoulders. When the eagle attacks you it will be unable to get its claws into the polystyrene and will fly off in despair whilst you leisurely photograph the Crowned Eagle to show friends back home.

It is not wise to feed eagles with left over bits of meat from the dinner you couldn't eat at the hotel. This just encourages them to attack human beings.

Tip For Your Trip

Pack a polystyrene cape for your trip and also wear a wide-brimmed black hat when in eagle country.

15 SNAKES

Snakes, similar to cats and humans like warmth. Snakes have a habit of slithering into your hotel bedroom when nobody is noticing, then sliding into your bed and between the sheets where it is nice and cosy. There they will remain until discovered. Or they will aim for an armchair and curl up underneath a cushion where they can stay sleeping for quite a few weeks.

Other favourite places include the insides of shoes and socks. Should you leave a drawer open then a snake will be very happy to slide up and into the soft lovely warmth of your underwear.

A fellow traveller once told me that he saw a cobra zig-zagging very quickly along the outside path towards his bedroom. Apparently snakes are not only attracted by the warmth of your hotel bedroom but also by certain smells that you leave in it.

Like elephants, snakes will not attack unless disturbed. However, most snakes in unusual countries are deadly and with one thrust their venomous fangs can kill you within thirty minutes, the normal time allowed to administer an antidote to prevent the onset of death. These antidotes are of course not normally available in unusual countries. The only places they are available are in countries where these snakes do not live but where research is done on them.

To prevent death by snakebite this is what you must do:

(a)   Never walk in bare feet along a path or in your hotel room

(b)   Always keep your ankles covered

(c)   Unmake and remake your bed before going to sleep

(d)   Unpack and repack all your clothes before getting dressed

(e)   Inspect every potential nook and cranny in your hotel
       bedroom to look for snakes

Cobras are very common and should you be lucky enough to discover one you should kill it immediately. You can do this by beating it precisely on top of its head at least fifty times with a baseball bat.

This is what the locals do.

When the cobra is dead you are in a position to make a lot of money.

(a) You should extract its venom and sell it to tourists as an aphrodisiac

(b) You should peel off its skin and sell it to a local craftsman to make a belt

(c) You should sell the remaining meat to a restaurant for use as a local delicacy (not so easy if the cobra has just eaten a rat)

Tip For Your Trip

Always carry a baseball bat with you.

16 BIRDS OF PARADISE

Most of us have this image of paradise on earth. It is a hotel and a large dazzling blue swimming pool close to the edge of a palm-fringed white beach with crystal clear waters and a coral reef beyond. It is very enticing.

The hotel will have a veranda where breakfast and other meals are served. In the morning you can have a coffee and croissant and gaze at the beautiful sea which later will marinate your body. In the evening you will sit on the veranda sipping a cocktail and have your breath taken away by the inflamed red sky as you watch the sun quickly drop beyond the horizon to be submerged by the sea, now black with night. Within minutes there might be a quiver of moonlight reflecting on the dark ocean to enrich your romantic memories.

This is paradise. It is paradise for birds too. They know that these hotels are too good to be true, exposed as they are to the elements with no windows. So birds sit on the rafters waiting for food. They don't have to wait long.

If you are a birdwatcher you can see them swoop down towards any morsel of food that has been left unattended on a table.

On one occasion I was the first down for breakfast. A waiter had just laid out the buffet including a table with a diverse range of stale breads, cardboard croissants and tasteless Danish pastries. As soon as the waiter's back was turned a flock of twenty sparrows descended from the rafters to alight on the breakfast buffet and peck at the bread.

I clapped them away and then complained to the restaurant manager. He was very cross with me when I suggested the hotel keep a resident cat to scare off the birds. "Don't you realise," he told me angrily, "that it is illegal to keep cats in restaurants? It is a risk to hygiene."

On another occasion, on a paradise island a couple of guests took plates of bread from the buffet and searched for a table near the beach. Having claimed their table they returned to the buffet to select their starters. By the time they returned the bread had been taken by birds.

In the natural world birds are breadwinners.

Tip For Your Trip

Avoid all carbohydrates on your trip (such as pastries, breads, cakes and cookies) – as the birds will have pecked at them first.

17 INSECTS

In Edward Wilson's brilliant book "*The Diversity of Life*" he states (pages 132-3) that there are 1.4 million species of living organisms on this earth, only half have been discovered and described.

Apparently, explorers are coming across previously undiscovered species of insects every day in Brazilian rain forests. You will also come across them in your hotel room in unusual countries.

Back home you will probably be familiar with only six types of insects: namely flies, ants, bees, wasps, beetles and spiders, although according to EU regulations the latter are no longer allowed to be classified as insects.

However, in unusual countries you will discover insects that even the locals know nothing about.

On a pillow in my hotel room I came across a revolting red creature with bulging eyes, long antennae and a horribly twisted deformed body. Nearby was an even more revolting black creature that looked like a cross between a beetle, a fly and a toothpick. Then there are a myriad of even smaller creatures of different hues that creep into your room, crawl up the wall and hide behind your bed to avoid being eaten by lizards.

When visiting unusual countries it could be a full-time job killing these insects (before they kill you). Positive thinking has an important role to play here. There are two positive thinking options.

OPTION ONE
Do nothing and trust that these insects will not harm you.

OPTION TWO
Capture the most unusual looking insects and put them into a small glass container. Take them back home and sell them to university lecturers who specialise in biodiversity so that their students can identify these insects in class. When they discover a brand new insect the professor will write a paper for a learned journal naming the new insect after himself and will become famous. There is a lucrative trade to be had here.

Tip For Your Trip

Purchase from a medical supplier, three specimen bottles in which you can place unusual insects that you capture. Pack them in your hand baggage. The empty bottles will also prove useful on aeroplanes when there are long queues for the toilet.

Whilst waiting in the queue for the toilet read a copy of Edward Wilson's book "*The Diversity of Life*" (Allen Lane 1993).

18 BED BUGS

Rest assured that in every bed in every hotel room in every unusual country there are at least ten thousand bed bugs.

Bed bugs really have a great life. They lie in bed all day long, wake up in the middle of the night for a virtual feast of the leftovers of your skin and the previous thousand people that have slept in the same bed.

When a photograph of one of these bed bugs is magnified one hundred times they look like some monster from outer space, with ugly reddish brown prickly bodies and huge horny things coming out of their heads. The sight of one is enough to frighten anyone.

One or two of the more adventurous of these bugs will crawl through the lining of your mattress, then through the holes in your sheets and then delicately bite your skin. These are the bugs who like their skin fresh. They do it with such immense finesse that for you the victim, the process of biting is quite painless. You will not know you have been bitten until you wake up in the morning and find your arms, back and bum covered in red blotches, most of which itch like Hell. By this time the bed bug will have escaped back into the mattress and will be snoring peacefully after such a great meal.

There are two simple solutions to prevent bed bugs attacking you. The first is to turn your mattress over. The brain of a bed bug has less than one megabyte of memory and it really does take him a very long time to work out what to do when his world is literally turned upside down. It confuses him immensely.

The second solution is to cover the mattress with a plastic sheet. You can buy these in any medical accessories shop. Incontinent people use them all the time so the shopkeeper will understand.

Tip For Your Trip

It is essential you purchase from your local medical supplies shop a plastic sheet especially designed for incontinent people. Pack this in your hand baggage. It is also quite useful on aeroplanes when there are long queues for the toilet.

19 ANTS

I encounter some really eccentric travelling companions. One of them had this unusual habit of waking up at 5:00 am every morning, doing ten minutes of strange breathing exercises, sipping a teaspoonful of his own urine and then drinking two glasses of warm water before lying naked on the floorboards for twenty minutes meditation during which time he repeated his own personal mantra (which I am not allowed to disclose).

One morning whilst meditating in an unusual country he experienced a strange tickling sensation on his right leg. He looked up to see a column of vicious looking ants rapidly approaching his private parts.

These ants were not the tiny little wimps you find back home, which run round aimlessly in any old direction that can be exterminated with a wet cloth. These were giant ants with glaring eyes and shiny black bodies. They were marching to order and to a strict sense of purpose. They were the sort of movie stars you find in a Pixar film.

He rushed to the shower only to find a trickle of water. He picked up his reserve bucket and flushed the ants away with this. However, they were not after Arthur at all. He was merely obstructing their main objective, a destination under his bed.

It was at that very moment that the earthquake occurred. The ants were already under the bed and Arthur joined them quickly. There was some minor damage as the walls cracked and the roof sagged perilously above them, but both the ants and Arthur survived to tell the story.

We human beings might have bigger brains but ants are far better equipped to detect impending earthquakes, volcanoes, tornados and hurricanes.

Next time you see a column of giant ants marching in your direction you know there is going to be a really big problem. When the world comes to an end it will be the ants who will be the first to know.

Tip For Your Trip

When you see a column of ants aiming for you, run! There's going to be a natural disaster!

Also pack in your hand baggage two wet sponges, one for each leg. Keep them wet in order to wash away ants in your (I'm sorry for the cliché) pants. They will also prove useful on aeroplanes when there are long queues for the toilet. Do not squeeze them out in public.

CHAPTER 2

FOOD AND HYGIENE IN UNUSUAL COUNTRIES

To maximise the chances of survival in unusual countries, regrettable as it might be, you simply have to eat the food provided. Whilst there is a fairly high risk of dying from this food there is a higher statistical probability of dying by not eating at all.

The next few sections will reveal the food that you are forced to consume in unusual countries is nothing like the food you enjoy at home. Whilst it occasionally does have the basic nutrients to keep your skin aglow and provides sufficient energy to walk during the day and have sex with the person of your choosing during the night, more often than not the food is totally devoid of any qualities you might expect food to have.

Personally, the occasions I have enjoyed a meal in an unusual country have been few. More often they have been awful. But I suppose when you are starving the enjoyment of fine food is hardly a requisite.

Part of the problem with food in unusual countries is hygiene. There is very little of it. This is one of the major cultural differences between unusual countries and those places you consider normal.

20 FOOD

I was brought up during the Second World War and we were grateful for bread, margarine, Spam and the occasional roast beef on a Sunday. More recently I have graduated to Mexican chimichangas, Indian chicken tikkas and Chinese aromatic duck.

Those of you with more adventurous tastes will be delighted to learn that an even wider variety of foods is available for you to savour in unusual countries. You can look forward to the following choices on the menus during your travels:

Birds And Bats

* Baby chicks boiled live in their shells just before they hatch
* Chicken beaks (in sauce)
* Chicken testicles (stewed in herbs)
* Raw eggs (to be poured over hot rice)
* Ostrich meat (roasted)
* Bats hearts (good for asthma)
* Owl (frizzled)

Beasts

* Live monkey brains (strap monkey in special hole in dining table, with head poking up)
* Raw horse meat very thinly sliced
* Cooked horse meat (passed off as 'meat')
* Smoked donkey
* Pigs intestines (copied from the French who call it 'andouille')
* Pigs feet (boiled)
* Pig skin and fat (braised)
* Various types of offal (normally fried)
* Tongues (very savoury when cold)
* Bulls testicles (often turned into pâte)
* Bulls penis (in cream sauce or fried)
* Cow skin (used to add gristle to a stew)
* The stomach lining of a cow (considered a load of tripe by many)
* Sheep stomach

* The tail of an ox (used in soups)
* Brains (a much favoured delicacy)
* An animal's pancreas (called 'ris de veau' by the French to make you think it is rice and veal)
* Fresh animal blood (often turned into puddings)
* Gorilla steaks (normally gorilled)
* Lion meat (very rare)
* Tiger steaks (T-bones)
* Bear paws (tenderised)
* Elephant trunks (served as soup)
* Elephant steaks
* Giraffe (roasted. A long table will be required for serving a whole roasted giraffe)
* Camel curry
* Armadillo (in a shell)
* Dog meat (used in meatballs - and very suitable at the end of the meal for 'doggy bags')
* Cat meat (used in savoury mince)
* Rabbits (used in goulashes)
* Bone marrow (used in jellies)
* Hedgehogs (baked whole in clay)
* Rats (normally served in prison)

Bugs, Crawlers And Slimy Creatures

* Various types of insects such as ants, locusts, grasshoppers (coated in chocolate)
* Cockroaches and beetles (good for snacking on)
* Scorpion (scorched)
* Snails (with garlic)
* Snail gonads (served as a starter on toast)
* Snake meat (goes well with salad)
* Frogs legs (in tomato sauce)
* Whole frogs (served in crispy batter with rice)
* Alligator or crocodile meat (turned into 'nuggets' or alternatively 'kebabs')

Fishy Stuff

* Lobsters cooked alive and served alive (with their antennae still twitching)
* Live prawns (on a very hot plate)
* Fish lips (with caviar)
* Fish intestines (uncooked)
* Raw fish bowels
* Cold shredded jellyfish
* Piranha salad
* Eels (normally with jelly)
* Sea slugs (sautéed and best served with cashew nuts)
* Sea turtles (butchered alive to stop the meat sticking to the shell)

Vegetarian

* Fresh seaweed (very good as a starter)
* Grass and weeds (used for tea and other infusions)
* Green chilli, red chilli and many other eye-watering spices
* Poisonous chemicals and colourings of every description (imported from the West and more fashionably described as hi-tech "e-food")

In people's quest for more exotic foods some of these dishes from unusual countries are of course now available where you live.

Tip For Your Trip

When eating local cuisine keep an open mind, an open mouth and a sick bag nearby. It's also best not to look at what you are eating let alone ask what it is.

21 HYGIENE

The concept of hygiene is of course a modern Western invention created by conventional doctors and pharmaceutical companies to keep them in business. If we ignored hygiene we would be healthier and doctors and drug giants would be out of business. This is what happens in unusual countries where few people go to doctors.

The trouble with hygiene is that it lowers the defences of your immune system making you more vulnerable to infection. Once you get an infection you go to the doctor (fee number one) who will send you to a pharmacist (fee number two) to obtain an antibiotic (fee number three, for the drug companies). Often there is a triple whammy because the doctors will also advise you to have a vaccination (fee number four). The paradox is that vaccinations are based on the same principle as 'lack of hygiene'. All vaccinations do is inject you with small quantities of the pathogens (poisons) that you have so studiously avoided by being hygienic.

There is a saying "that a little bit of dirt does you good." This lesson is drawn from animals that eat small amounts of their own faeces. This provides them with invaluable bacteria and also stimulates their immune system to keep them healthy. However this is not to be recommended for human beings.

Having said that, there is a growing practice in some countries to drink a small amount of your own urine every morning. They say this is very good for you. I haven't tried it yet, preferring a good cup of English breakfast tea.

Summarily you should not worry too much about hygiene in unusual countries.

Once your immune system has adjusted to life in these places you will find yourself as fit and healthy as the locals. In the interim period of six months you will suffer from an inordinate number of ailments such as stomach disorders, skin rashes, facial infections and mouth ulcers.

Tip For Your Trip

Never wash your hands in unusual countries, you never know where the water's been.

22 HASHISH CAKES

Cake warning!

Do not eat cakes in unusual countries. You have been warned! They look terrific but taste terrible. The cakes will have the allure of primary colour icing and primary colour fillings. But that is all. Once you start eating the incredibly small portions served you will find them totally insipid. They are like tasteless soggy mousses. It is rare to find a cake of any substance like the succulent fruitcake my nana used to prepare or the delicious crunchy apple crumble my mum used to make.

There is a hidden danger too which necessitates this essential cake warning. I will quote from a national newspaper I was reading one morning in an unusual country:

HASHISH OIL USED IN CAKES

If that piece of brownie you're eating is giving you an unusual high, one of its ingredients might just be hashish oil, according to the National Bureau of Investigation (NBI). Operatives of the NBI have received information that marijuana farmers have been mixing the plant extract, also called hashish oil, with baked goods like cakes and cookies.

These farmers reportedly bake the brownies and cakes at their marijuana plantations and then sell them in towns in the lowlands. Only recently have the farmers learnt how to extract hashish oil. Before they used dried marijuana leaves as one of the ingredients in baking their special cakes and brownies.

According to the news item this fashion is catching on and you could eat a cake anywhere nowadays and get on a high. This is highly dangerous because you could become addicted to cakes whilst travelling in these countries.

Tip For Your Trip

Do not eat cakes in unusual countries!

23 HOSPITALITY

The whole point of travelling is not just to visit popular tourist sites in order to buy postcards to send home but to meet interesting people. People who are interesting are of the type you've never met before. In other words they tend to be strangers and mainly local. Their habits will be different to yours and they will eat unusual foods. Their approach to hygiene is unusual too. I know local people who will spend twenty minutes cleaning their teeth with a flayed twig under a standpipe tap. The locals with buckets in the queue behind never complain.

Ninety-nine per cent of people in unusual countries are also incredibly hospitable. There are two general rules of thumb which apply to this hospitality:

(a) The poorer the people are the more hospitable they become.

(b) The further you are from a big city the more hospitable people will be.

I have been overwhelmed by the hospitality shown to me by people I have met in unusual countries. They have invited me to their homes, introduced me to their grannies, their kids and their goats and devoted an inordinate amount of time to showing me around. They have even told me the truth about their country (normally that the President is corrupt and exploits innocent helpless people like them).

One of the things you learn from local people is that you don't have to be rich to be happy. It is something you always knew but found difficult to accept back home. A family I know is lucky to earn two dollars a day. Most days they only eat rice and they are more than happy to share that rice with me (I normally take some chicken along with me so that helps).

Back home many of us are totally selfish and totally consumed with material greed. Thus we rarely have time to look after visitors and make them feel welcome.

The lesson I have learned is that if people offer you hospitality in an unusual country always accept it. Always drink that foul-tasting tea with herbs in it, always eat that foul-looking food that they have spooned on to the plate for you, always accept their gifts no matter how inappropriate they are. And accept their hygiene too.

Outside the hut of one family I was with, a cubicle enclosed the toilet. This toilet had no seat let alone a bowl. There was merely a gutter in the ground at which to aim. When finished I had to pick up a pan, dip it into a large drum of water and flush away along the gutter my own effluent. It disappeared into a bigger hole at the end of the street. Needless to say my friends' toilet cubicle was spotlessly clean which was more than could be said for my socks and trousers.

Tip For Your Trip

Always take with you a selection of small gifts. (I take lots and lots of shiny pens with my name on).

24 RESTAURANTS

Restaurants in unusual countries are there for one reason only: to test your patience and level of tolerance.

Whilst at home you might be used to fast food, in unusual countries the tendency is towards slow food or at worst food that never comes. You should schedule at least three hours for any meal. For example, here is a typical lunch timetable:

1:00 pm	Arrive at restaurant with party of four.
1:05 pm	Sit at table. Drinks orders taken. Menus presented.
1:25 pm	Drinks arrive. All drinks have ice in them when each guest stated "No ice". One guest asked for diet cola but received ordinary cola (because in this country they call it 'cola-light' and the waiter didn't understand).
1:30 pm	Waiter takes order for starters and main course but points out that most items are not available. However, they do have a speciality of the day (which is very expensive). Unwilling to offend the waiter each person orders the speciality of the day together with a starter.
2:00 pm	Glasses are empty. No sign of food. No sign of waiter.
2:05 pm	Starters arrive but they are not what was ordered. The waiter is completely confused and just puts the plates in front of each diner anyway. Unwilling to offend the waiter each person eats the dish he or she has not ordered. More drinks are ordered.
2:30 pm	Drinks arrive. The waiter does not notice that each diner has finished the starter and the plates are dirty. He disappears without removing the dirty plates.
2:45 pm	Speciality dish arrives. The waiter leaves it on a separate table whilst clearing the dirty plates. The speciality dish gets cold. It is undercooked.
2:50 pm	Unwilling to offend the waiter each person eats the speciality. It is not special.
3:00 pm	Restaurant manager arrives with beaming smile. He shakes everyone's hand and asks "Is everything all right?" Are you enjoying the lunch?" Everyone smiles, nods and tells the manager the lunch is wonderful.
3:30 pm	Waiter removes the dirty plates. The party of four decides against dessert and coffee. The bill is asked for.

3:45 pm   The bill comes. It is not itemised. The amount seems excessive. An itemised bill is asked for. It comes. It is wrong. The party has been charged for items it didn't have. The manager has disappeared. The waiter doesn't understand. Unwilling to offend the waiter the bill is settled. It has come to £20 for four people (including drinks) when it should have been £16. Someone leaves a £4 tip for good service.

4:00 pm   Leave restaurant.

Meanwhile it is advisable not to use the strange toilets in these restaurants for the simple reason that the restaurant staff are far too busy to clean them. Nor should you ask to visit the kitchen because they will not want you to see the cockroach infestation, the greasy walls and the rotting meat in the fridge.

Tip For Your Trip

Allow plenty of time for your meal and do not expect good service.

Always check your order and check the bill.

Take a fan with you to flick away the flies that will descend on your food.

25 BREAKFAST

You can forget breakfast, at least as you know it. Normally there are two types of breakfast: the one you have at home and the one you have in hotels. Neither is available in unusual countries.

There are many unusual countries where locals tend to eat rice and fish for breakfast if not watery porridge (sometimes called congee) or mealy-meal. They have no idea about proper breakfast. So the hotels in unusual countries thus concoct an artificial breakfast especially for Westerners. By this I mean imitation bacon, simulated sausages, faked scrambled eggs and that's if you are lucky. The bacon will look like and taste like shredded striped cardboard. The sausages will be like frankfurters but taste of pepper and paste, whilst the eggs will be either gelatinous or powdery.

Sometimes there will be no attempt at hot breakfast and merely a selection of cold meats and tropical fruits which have been standing for hours for flies to walk over.

You have to face it, in most of these places they do not even know how to make toast. It always ends up tasting like a baby's rusk. Furthermore, tea will taste like boiled water and the coffee like cough syrup. I have had tea based on the principles of homeopathy.

Bread rolls will come in one size and colour only, none of this fancy stuff such as granary rolls, rye bread and so on. If there is any butter it will be in little aluminium tablets designed to spread butter all over your fingers as you open them. Jam will be available as a microfilm in skinny little tubs that are impossible to open. This jam will be devoid of fruit and is normally chemically coloured jelly.

In most unusual countries there is only one choice of cereal and that will be cornflakes which have the consistency of pencil shavings. Some more progressive hotels have introduced branflakes in the interests of health, but these branflakes other than being a little darker in colour, taste exactly the same as the cornflakes. In other words they taste terrible. If there is milk (and there isn't always) it will be that cotton-woolly sterilised type. Often it is off.

Sometimes there is a choice of fruit juices but these will always taste like the old fashioned lemon or orange squash we used to drink after the war. I tried some orange juice in an unusual country recently and it tasted of disinfectant. It was ghastly.

Tip For Your Trip

If you insist on eating breakfast in an unusual country only eat bread rolls with a little butter (if you can hunt it down). Also, only drink tea because you know the water has almost been boiled. The other option is to lose weight.

26 WATER

It is a fact that the water you get through the taps in unusual countries is not quite up to the quality of the water you get at home.

This is because it is not meant to be drunk by foreigners. You can bathe in it, even risk cleaning your teeth in it but do not dare drink it even if there is a notice in the hotel bathroom to the contrary.

Sometimes water suppliers give you a nice big clue and the water comes out of the tap a rather murky brown colour. It is then obvious you should not drink it let alone bathe in it. More frequently however the water is deceptively clear and might even taste deceptively nice. However, do not be taken in. You should not allow a drop to pass your gullet for there is ninety-nine per cent chance that your stomach will object and you will pass the night, not in sleep, but passing unpleasant liquids down the toilet.

The locals might argue otherwise telling you that their tap water is perfectly safe and clean. But this is because their stomachs are accustomed to the germs and the poisons that commonly exist in their water supply. Your stomach is definitely not attuned and will definitely react.

Your top priority on arriving at your destination is to acquire a bottle of mineral water. There are two types: the inexpensive and the expensive. The inexpensive is local mineral water and the expensive is imported from Europe. Usually the local mineral water is safe but do make sure the top has not been tampered with and they haven't refilled an empty bottle with tap water. It is advisable to find a local shop to purchase mineral water as the hotel will charge you thirty times as much.

Tip For Your Trip

Carry water purifying tablets with you.

27 LOCAL WINES

Most unusual countries have begun to realise that the world beyond them is full of alcoholics. With one or two rare exceptions you can't go anywhere in the world without seeing people drinking alcohol. In restaurants, in bars, on aeroplanes, in trains, at home everywhere you will see people consuming various types and amounts of this life-threatening liquid.

Unusual countries have therefore started producing some of the most life-threatening wines that you will ever come across. Most local people are so poor they cannot afford to drink these wines (they stick to their tried and tested local star beers) and therefore do not know how bad these wines can be. In other words, because of the high prices of these wines they are only offered to visitors.

When offered such a wine you will be informed authoritatively that these local wines are as good as any produced in Europe, California or Australia. You will take a sip, smile and nod in agreement. However, first impressions are deceptive and you will find the taste deteriorating with every mouthful and your stomach churning as the vinegar works its way through your system.

Furthermore, local wines are full of deadly chemicals which cause dreadful hangovers. I've been told that you can drink a whole bottle of classy French champagne and not get a hangover. The reverse is true with local wines, one glass is enough to give you a throbbing hangover even before you start the second glass.

Regrettably. it is rude to refuse wine when offered and unless you have established a long campaign trail to prove you are teetotal you will have to drink at least one glass and suffer the consequences.

There is one antidote which is partially effective and this is milk. It lines your stomach. You should therefore consume at least half-a-litre of milk before risking a glass of local wine. However, milk is not always available in unusual countries. After drinking wine consume as much mineral water as possible.

Tip For Your Trip

Take with you on the aeroplane a carrier bag containing six half-litre cartons of long-life milk and three litres of mineral water.

28 CLUB SANDWICHES

A staple diet for many travellers around the world is the club sandwich. It is a stupid name for a sandwich because very few people eat it in clubs. However, you will find it available in almost every hotel in the world.

There are various standards of club sandwich some of which are far from acceptable. It is always wise therefore to take your own recipe along with you so that you can advise the head chef (alias the hotel manager, alias the head of housekeeping, alias the barman) how to prepare this delicacy in accordance with your own exacting standards.

Here is the recipe for the 'international' (unusual countries) version:

1. Take three slices of bread (any OLD bread will do, never use fresh bread).

2. Toast it slightly so that it hardens to the texture of cardboard.

3. Scrape a little mayonnaise on to the toasted bread and then scrape off again. Take care not to use too much. Never use margarine let alone butter, this would be unforgivable.

4. Add two bits of bacon, one between each gap (leftover bits from breakfast are by far the best. The colder and the older the better).

5. Slip in two or three slices of boiled egg (any type of old egg: pigeon egg, duck egg, the customer won't know the difference).

6. Scatter everywhere small chunks of leftover chicken (or turkey, or whatever is available).

7. Pad out the gaps with unwashed lettuce sparsely decorated with a very thin slice or two of tomato.

8.   Compress the completed club sandwich with your hands (don't bother to wash them) and cut into four triangles.

9. Stack the four triangles into a neat pyramid and spear with two toothpicks.

10. Garnish the plate with a few crisps, chips or French fries and a quarter of overripe tomato if you can find one.

11. Serve cold and late. The hungrier the customer is the more he or she will enjoy it.

12. Charge at least $US17 (the higher the price the more the customer will value the sandwich).

Tip For Your Trip

Always present a copy of this recipe to the waiter when ordering a club sandwich. If necessary try to negotiate down the price.

29 SUPERMARKETS

It would be ignorance of the highest order to assume that unusual countries do not have supermarkets. They do. You can smell them a mile off. Normally the smell is of old cheese, dead fish and rotting vegetables. As soon as you step inside these supermarkets this foul odour is all-pervasive albeit your nose quickly adapts.

Beggars are attracted to this smell too and wait outside supermarkets for the odd coin you might toss them from the change given to you at the counter. On one occasion a beggar followed me all the way back from the supermarket entrance to where the car was parked half-a-mile away (it is difficult to park outside a supermarket entrance – even in unusual countries). This beggar didn't even offer to carry the four bags of shopping I had. Nor did he open the car door for me. This was because he had no arms and was on crutches. He also only had one leg working properly.

Returning to the subject of supermarkets most of those in unusual countries are compact and are the size of your average corner shop in the UK – it makes them very easy to get around. The prices are either amazingly low or amazingly high depending on whether it's local produce or imported.

In addition to the smells, the noise from squeaking grocery carts can also be immensely irritating. These small trolleys are used so much that they are rusting away, bent, battered and full of bits of litter.

In the interests of health most of these supermarkets sell fresh fruit and vegetables. Basically there are two types of this essential nutrition: the cheap local produce covered in dirt and the expensive imported produce covered in polystyrene to hide the dirt.

Other features of these remarkably progressive supermarkets are the low lighting (in the interests of preventing global warming), rustic flooring and the limited range of everything. In a supermarket I once visited there was only one brand of condensed milk available. In fact there was only one tin of condensed milk available. It's used in tea – as fresh milk is not available.

The checkout staff were friendly enough, although they refused to take my credit card. I therefore had to pay in cash – a big thick wad of local currency coming to at least ten dollars in exchange value.

Tip For Your Trip

Always wear nose plugs and drench yourself in perfume before entering a supermarket in an unusual country. Expect to pay cash.

30 STRANGE TOILETS Part I

It will come as a shock to the system to most people reading this book but 99.9% of the people living in this world do not have toilets as we know them. In fact, the flushing toilet we so fondly clean back home was only invented in the nineteenth century. Before that it was all chamber pots, piss pots, backs of trees and behind the bushes. In many unusual countries flushing toilets have still not caught on.

The end result is that many people in unusual countries are still using the same type of toilet that Adam and Eve used, namely a hole in the ground. The 'après-toilette' technique is almost identical to the one used by a cat or boy scouts at camp: you scoop some dirt over the mess you've made. The leaves from certain bushes can also come in quite useful here (see section on TOILET PAPER). Alternatively, you scoop up some water from a barrel and douse yourself down before throwing further pans of water at the effluent to flush it away.

In some unusual countries there have been major advances and the hole in the ground is surrounded by white tiles although they will not be white when you arrive as many people miss the hole. To help overcome the problem of 'missing the hole' a hose is provided and you are meant to wash away any spattered spillages into it. Most users of these toilets fail to do this for the simple reason that no water ever comes out of the hose. (Perhaps they have hosepipe bans too).

The use of holes explains why men in many countries do not wear trousers. Western men have immense difficulty in protecting the trousers around their ankles from straying particles.

It is therefore essential that you are effectively 'potty trained' before being confronted with a 'pothole in the ground' or 'gutter' toilet in an unusual country. This is easy. Back home you should dig a pothole two feet deep and six inches square in your garden or back yard. Erect a tent around this hole to give you some privacy whilst practising. If you live in an apartment use the local park.

Before practising you need to undertake two weeks of 'squatting exercises' in your bathroom to strengthen your thighs and stomach muscles (this is good for you anyway). To do this, stand carefully on your toilet seat and balance yourself. Then place your ankles eighteen inches apart, raise your heels slightly and then crouch such that your buttocks are approximately fourteen inches from the toilet seat. This is the perfect position. Practice this 'squat and crouch' routine twenty times a day for a week. Then practice using the pothole you have dug.

Tip For Your Trip

It is best to practice with 'hole-in-the-ground' toilets for several weeks at home first. However if you do not develop sufficient prowess you should take with you on your trip an extra pair of trousers, two extra pairs of underwear and three damp J Cloths.

31 OFFICE TOILETS

As indicated in previous sections, toilets can dominate the thought process of visitors to unusual countries. This section is for readers who are brave enough to go and work in these countries and then with the customary lack of foresight, decide to use the office toilets.

They will immediately discover that 'toilet etiquette' in such places is highly unusual. For starters they will not be able to get into the office toilet. It will be locked.

Part of the power base of any senior manager is to hold the key to the office toilet. This means you have to go and interrupt his meeting to politely request him for it. Most local bosses are sufficiently understanding when you point to your crotch and then the toilet along the corridor. They will grunt and thrust the key at you whilst continuing their important meeting. The problem arises when you have a weak bladder or are suffering from the inevitable 'loose bowel' syndrome. This will necessitate innumerable visits every morning not only to the toilet but to the boss first.

The next problem you will find is that there is no toilet paper in the toilet. This is why 'management' keep the toilet under lock and key, to prevent people stealing toilet paper. It is stolen anyway – probably by managers.

It is also highly unlikely that you will find any soap, towels (paper or otherwise) in the toilet. If there is a hot air blower it will not work for more than five seconds (like those back home).

To minimise your number of visits to the toilet during working hours I would suggest that prior to setting out for the office you....

(a)   .... do not drink coffee (a purgative)

(b)   .... do not drink tea (a diuretic)

(c)   .... do not drink juice (which turns the stomach)

(c)   .... do not drink water (which impacts both the bladder and bowel)

(d)   .... do not eat breakfast (which makes you feel bad anyway)

Furthermore, you should avoid lunch and thus impress the local boss and all his team about your commitment to working long hard hours.

Tip For Your Trip

It should be your top priority to pack at least six rolls of luxury toilet paper for your trip and always carry one roll with you in your briefcase or jacket pocket. I cannot stress how important this is.

The only other option is to go on a 24 hour fast prior to visiting any office in an unusual country.

32 BAD FOOD

It is generally accepted that much of the food in unusual countries is bad. This is for a variety of reasons. Vegetables and fruit are grown in sewage which is not washed off afterwards. Refrigeration practices are enough to make you come out in a sweat. Furthermore (see section on HYGIENE) there is no attention to hygiene as people are unfamiliar with the concept. Meat is generally exposed to flies and other insects. Hands are never washed, especially after going to the toilet, as there are no toilets to speak of. Deliveries are slow and unreliable and this means that most food has to hang around much longer than normal.

The end result is:

*   Sour milk
*   Mouldy cheese
*   Bruised apples
*   Rotting tomatoes
*   Cans of food past their sell-by date
*   Stale bread (and pastries and cakes)
*   Meat of questionable origin and of unquestionably awful taste and toughness
*   Meat that has not been cooked properly
*   Bottles of mineral water that have been refilled with tap water
*   Tap water that has not been treated to remove bacteria and traces of sewage
*   Fish that has the overpowering smell of fish
*   Other food that has the overpowering smell of fish
*   Green vegetables coated in unspeakable grime and dirt
*   Other vegetables of indeterminate variety
*   Chickens that have no flesh and are all skin and bone
*   Bananas (or plantains) that have gone all squidgy
*   Coffee that is not the real thing and has been doctored with imitation coffee (dirt)
*   Ice cream that is a breeding ground for bacteria
*   Tea that has no taste

*   Greasy plates and dirty knives and forks
*   Colas and soda waters that are flat
*   Fruit juices that are fermenting
*   Wine that is literally acid

Tip For Your Trip

If you insist on eating food whilst visiting an unusual country then stick with rice. In fact, the stickier the rice the better. The local beer is normally okay too.

Alternatively, you might consider taking a stomach pump with you. The manual version is quite good (sticking two fingers down your throat).

You should avoid any food that has been pre-masticated by the head chef or tribal chief – or any food that has been diluted with spittle.

33 SMELLS

Even if you are blind and deaf you can identify an unusual country by its unique smells or, to be less polite, by the unusual way it stinks.

This is not being rude because Britain stinks too. But we Brits are so used to our own odious smells we do not notice.

Thus a visitor from abroad would actually die from nasal shock if he were to enter the dressing room immediately after an English rugby match and experience the stench. Furthermore, entering an English pub at closing time can destroy the nostrils of a foreigner.

In other words the smells in unusual countries are different.

For a start, the highly spiced food people eat in unusual countries contributes to a type of body odour and halitosis which is much more noticeable than the pong you get from your family and friends — even when they eat pickled onions or garlic bread. So never get close to local people (poor or rich) in unusual countries. They smell terrible!

Furthermore, you will find the streets in unusual countries smell differently. The stench emanating from the blocked drains and frequent piles of rubbish on street corners will knock you back and you will find it difficult to breathe for a few brief seconds. The street smells are often so foul it is as if there are rotting carcasses below each drain. There probably are.

Even hotels in unusual countries have a unique stench. In one hotel I noticed a distinctive smell as I walked from the elevator along the corridor to my bedroom. It was some special blend of cigarette smoke, disinfectant and perfume of wild roses. I think it was an attempt to disguise the smell of piss which I could just detect with my hypersensitive nose.

Restaurants are the same. They are full of fetid odours. It might be dampness, it might be stale food, it might be the urine leaking out of the toilets, or it might be because the waiters are not very efficient at cleaning vomit from the floor

– but overall there is a distinctive smell about restaurants in unusual countries that makes you not want to eat in them. But of course you have to – so your nose quickly adapts, being subordinate to the stomach.

Tip For Your Trip

Before venturing out anaesthetise your nose by drenching your face in strong perfume or aftershave. Alternatively have a fag (see section on SMOKING) – so take ten duty free packs of cigarettes with you.

34 TOILET PAPER

I was advised by a local ranger that rhinoceros mark the boundaries of their territory with fresh dung. Other animals do so too although human beings tend not to, even in unusual countries.

With so much rhinoceros dung around going for a stroll on a pleasant Sunday afternoon in the unusual countryside can prove quite hazardous. It is therefore wise to have a roll of toilet paper with you. However, most of us don't think of this before going for a walk. In unusual countries you cannot expect to find a corner shop in the middle of the country let alone a petrol station which sells toilet paper.

As usual mother nature has the perfect answer to help those of you who mess up your shoes by stepping in the wrong place or are in danger of messing up your pants by eating the wrong foods – and it is not a soft fluffy roll of your favourite toilet paper.

Nature's answer is in the form of a tree called the 'weeping wattle'. This tree grows wild in many unusual countries and offers the most cost-effective form of toilet paper you will ever find. Its leaves are large, strong, soft and silky as well as incredibly absorbent. In fact, indigenous people have been using these leaves for the purposes of sanitation since the year dot.

When there is a call of nature, or they want to wipe their feet free of rhinoceros dung they just hop across to the nearest weeping wattle tree and grab a few leaves. It is as simple as that.

Well not quite.

The weeping wattle is a member of the acacia family and grows in the vicinity of acacia trees which tend to look similar. However, there is one fundamental difference if you make a mistake in identification. The acacia tree is full of thorns and its leaves are very very prickly.

Tip For Your Trip

Always carry six rolls of fluffy toilet paper with you.

CHAPTER 3

MEDICAL AND MATTERS RELATED TO SEX IN UNUSUAL COUNTRIES

I really am sorry, but if you suffer from hypochondria or paranoia you should never visit an unusual country. Anyone with a nervous disposition, a tendency towards hysteria or an obsession with health should stay at home and watch reality television. The same applies if you want 'safe sex' in unusual countries. There is no such thing (and I'm not talking about disease).

In unusual countries conventions relating to medicine, health and sex deviate widely from our strange practices back home.

My late grandmother epitomised the medical beliefs that are now prevalent in unusual countries. She lived to ninety-four and for a start didn't believe in doctors. In her view if you went to see a doctor he would find something wrong with you. So she avoided seeing doctors. Furthermore she didn't believe in hospitals. "More people die in hospitals than anywhere else," she was always telling me. Until the day she died she never went to hospital. Very wise!

People in unusual countries tend to have the same beliefs, but for different reasons – as you will discover in the forthcoming sections.

35 MEDICAL SUPPLIES

Only the most ignorant and inexperienced travellers to unusual countries will fail to take a handy kit of essential medical supplies with them.

The 'law of perversity in adversity' dictates that the thing that you are least prepared for will happen to you. Mercifully it is not difficult to acquire essential medicines before departing for one of these countries.

Here is a list of the things I normally forget to take:

* Ammonia
* Antacid indigestion tablets
* Antibiotics (generic)
* Antidandruff shampoo
* Antihistamines and inhalers
* Antiseptic foot powder and creams
* Antiseptic liquids
* Anti snake-bite serum
* Aspirin (or equivalent)
* Baby wipes (or wet tissues)
* Bandages (enough for six big wounds)
* Blank prescription forms
* Chlorine solution
* Condoms (at least 60: this way you can discard the defective ones with holes in)
* Cotton wool and cotton buds
* Cream to put on insect bites
* Disinfectant
* Eye drops
* Garlic tablets
* Homeopathic remedies (for alternative solutions)
* Iodine
* Lozenges for sore throats
* Malaria tablets
* Medicinal alcohol (has other uses too)
* Medicinal red wine (has other uses too)

* Mouthwash and gargle liquid
* Pills to stop diarrhoea
* Plasters (variety pack)
* Rubber bands (different sizes)
* Safety pins, needles and syringes
* Scissors
* Sick bags (obtainable on your aeroplane)
* Six bottles of sterilised water
* Six cartons of long-life milk
* Six litres of whisky
* Sleeping tablets
* Sticky labels and a pen
* String (at least six meters)
* Swiss army knife
* Toenail clipper
* Tooth extractor
* Toothpicks
* Transparent plastic bags
* Vaseline
* Vitamin supplements

Tip For Your Trip

Using the above as a checklist, carefully prepare a first aid kit to take with you on your visit to an unusual country. Ensure every item above is included.

36 SEX PROBLEMS (Part 1)

Unusual countries are not like the West where you only have to smile at a member of the opposite sex for them to fall into bed with you.

Such behaviour is frowned upon, quite rightly, in unusual countries.

The thing to do is not to do it. Should you ever act upon your rampant impulses and are discovered then you will be in real trouble, not just immediately but for the rest of your life.

Therefore, be extremely careful when conversing with a stunningly beautiful member of the opposite sex in an unusual country, especially a local person. Use minimal eye contact, avoid body language at all times - body language is translated differently in different countries. Also, never make any suggestive remarks and be careful with jokes. Finally, never be personal with a member of the opposite sex. The only thing you should ever talk about is work and the country you are visiting. Politics, religion and privates lives are also completely out.

However, if you are really determined to pursue romance and adventure in an unusual country (in other words have sex with a beautiful local person) then select your potential partner wisely. Before jumping into bed with this person always ask the permission of this persons' parents. Everything can be arranged, at a price.

The normal price for such sex is marriage and total responsibility for the rest of your life for your new spouse's family (which will be larger than you ever realised).

You can be assured that after two years the novelty will have worn off and your sex problems will be even greater.

Tip For Your Trip

Avoid casual sex in unusual countries unless of course you want to live dangerously and create problems for the rest of your life. Just in case, take with you at least sixty strawberry flavoured ribbed condoms.

37 SEX PROBLEMS (Part 2)

Sex problems in unusual countries are created because many people who catch your eye ....

1. .... look stunning and are much more attractive than the run-of-the-mill people you occasionally get sexually attracted to back home

2. .... give you the impression that they are attracted to you (which never happens to people you are attracted to back home)

3. .... are actually interested in what you say and make you feel important

4. .... are definitely more exotic, enticing, fascinating and exciting than the sexual drone who is your current spouse/partner

5. .... are more charming, friendly and caring than anyone you normally meet

6. .... dress far better than the person who currently undresses for you

7. .... speak more languages than you or your partner does

8. .... are the types your friends have affairs with and you would iike to

9. .... keep thinner, fitter and have bodies more beautiful than you've ever seen before

10. .... appreciate you more than your current spouse/partner does

On the down side:

1. They will demand you take them to London (a city almost everyone in the world wants to visit) – or at least sponsor their visit so they can get a visa

2. Once you've fallen in love with them they can be bloody difficult

3. Once they 'hook' you they can make your life a misery

4. They will never let you leave them

5. You will be required (as mentioned in the previous section) to support their incredibly large extended family

There is a famous old saying that "the grass is greener on the other side". This definitely applies to the beautiful people you meet in unusual countries.

Tip For Your Trip

Assess the level of risk in seducing a person from an unusual country.

One night in bed can lead to a lifetime of misery. That's the risk.

Alternatively, one night in bed with a person from an unusual country can extract you from your current misery.

38 ACCIDENT AND EMERGENCY SERVICES

It is advisable not to have an accident in an unusual country. If you are prone to this type of thing then it is best to stay at home where they can amputate your leg fairly efficiently or restart your heart with the minimum of fuss.

Whilst local people will deny that accidents take place you will see from the number of burnt out cars on the sides of roads that they actually take place quite frequently.

Normally, if an accident occurs people will stand around and watch. I have also heard horror stories of passengers being burnt alive inside a minibus on a mountain pass and other traffic overtaking and accelerating away to avoid the screams.

If you do have an accident and are lucky enough to find some locals who are prepared to do something about it they will normally drag you unceremoniously from the wreck, throw you into the back seat of the first car that comes along and tell the driver to go as fast as possible to the hospital. Now this I have seen happen.

When the emergency services are called it can be pure theatre. They like to put on a good show (screaming sirens and flashing lights) but tend to fail on every other performance indicator. Few people have any confidence in them.

I visited one fire station a year or so back and actually found three unwashed fire engines. The first one had no wheels on (seriously!) and was propped up by wooden blocks placed under the wheel hubs. The second fire engine had a smashed windscreen and did not look as if it had been used in years. There was one very old decrepit red fire engine which I imagined might just struggle to life in the event of a fire. I wanted to ask the station commander about this but I could not find him. Nor could I find any crew. The station was completely unmanned at that point in time. However, my host assured me that this was one of the main fire stations in this capital city.

Furthermore, you would not recognise ambulances in some of these countries. They do not look like ambulances. They have flashing lights to sustain an element of machismo but most of them look like minibuses or pick-up trucks. I have seen people hailing an ambulance by mistake, thinking it was a local bus.

The police are even worse. They drive around in dark glasses in dark blue cars staring at every pretty young woman on the street. Often they sport guns and take care not to shave to make sure they have a real macho appearance. The police in unusual countries only have two objectives. The first is to chat up pretty women and the second is to take money off you if they can conjure up an offence. It is pointless reporting a robbery because most robbers are in collusion with the police.

Tip For Your Trip

Always have a contingency plan as to what to do in the case of an accident.

Take with you a first aid kit. It will come in handy. (See the section on MEDICAL SUPPLIES for a list of what to take).

39 HOSPITALS

You have seen pictures on television: a lot of heroic doctors and nurses tending injured and ill people in squalid hospitals with inadequate supplies. Not all hospitals in unusual countries are like this. Many do not even have heroic doctors and nurses.

Most public hospitals in unusual countries do not have adequate supplies of anything. If you can't get a decent cup of tea in these countries it is not surprising that there is often a shortage of anaesthetics, clean bandages and syringes – as well as a shortage of good doctors and nurses. No wonder the patients scream.

The medical staff that remain are often arrogant and treat the patients who dare to call upon their services with total disdain and disrespect. This tradition goes back to the good old colonial days when the boot was on the other foot.

In many of the hospitals staff consider themselves so important that nobody would even demean themselves to clean the toilets. Patients wee in the beds and on the floors anyway – just like any other country.

Summarily these public hospitals are best avoided, which is easier done than said – because you will find it difficult to get into them, given the crowds of potential patients that block the entrances and then queue for ages (days on end) for a routine vasectomy. I have heard stories of people making sure they get to hospitals at 3:00 am in the morning to ensure they get the first place in the queue for any operation going.

The exceptions are the small private hospitals which some foreign communities have had built in order to avoid the atrocious public hospitals. These are of a much higher quality in every sense. They even have clean floors and working toilets.

It is well worth researching all this before you visit an unusual country so that you know exactly where to go when you suffer a heart attack or fall under a bus.

Tip For Your Trip

Have a private air ambulance standing-by at the nearest airport just in case you suddenly get ill or have an accident. It will then be quite simple to fly home for treatment under the NHS (albeit you might have to wait ages in the A&E department). When you eventually do get to meet our wonderful doctors and nurses you will find they come from the same country you've just visited. So you will have a lot to talk about.

Ensure you have with you at all times a letter confirming that a private air-ambulance is standing-by.

40 SUN WORSHIPPERS

Forget all those wonderful advertisements, scrap your fantasies and get real. The sun is a killer!

Some while back I was in a very hot country and it was 38°C in the shade. I saw ageing Caucasian ladies return from the pool having baked themselves alive around it. They were suffering delusions that their decrepit old husbands would find them more attractive with their brown crinkled sagging breasts peeling to reveal large revolting swathes of blotchy red and white skin. Ugh! I never knew breasts could make you sick.

Even the younger marginally more attractive ones were deluding themselves. As I sipped my iced lemon tea in the coffee shop I could see them on the pool-side loungers roasting their skins away. Boy were they going to suffer! They had looked horrible at breakfast and looked far worse by the afternoon. They would be scratching themselves to death all night. There is no way I find all this overheated flesh sexy.

I will probably get lynched alive by the Mafioso of the travel industry but sun worshippers are on a mass suicide drive. Skin cancer is all the rage and tourists can't get enough of it.

It goes back to pagan times when people knew how to worship the sun properly, but now we modern human beings have lost the art. We are pretty crass at cooking ourselves alive. There are better ways of making human sacrifices and our ancestors knew how to do it.

I can never quite understand why people want a tan. What's wrong with being white? Skin colour has no relevance when it comes to inner beauty and spiritual health let alone physical fitness and sexual attraction.

The paradox is that if you visit pharmacists in many hot countries you will find a wide range of soaps, lotions and creams to whiten dark skin. This is an example from the label of one of these products: "BLOCK n WHITE: Enjoy the goodness of milk as it whitens your skin with the New Block & White Milk Whitening Lotion with a unique Triple Action formula."

Tip For Your Trip

Avoid vacations where the sun is hot, the sky is blue and there are white beaches, palm trees and crystal clear seas. These are the entry points to hell and the devil's way of preparing you for the hot flames you'll find there.

41 SMOKING

Recommendation: start smoking!

Whilst I am against smoking in principle it is highly recommended in unusual countries with many useful purposes that far outweigh the many disadvantages which will catch up with you later in life.

As you will have read previously, tobacco smoke is exceptionally valuable in warding off insects carrying deadly diseases. The choice is yours: do you want to die of dengue fever today or of lung cancer in thirty years time?

However, smoking has many other valuable benefits that are not widely promoted because of the invidious propaganda campaign that is being conducted by the 'anti smoking' press barons (who failed to invest in tobacco companies many years ago).

For example, when you visit unusual countries you will come across many people who smell absolutely awful. These locals will of course think the same about you. The reason is that people in other countries have different chemicals in their sweat glands. Smoking solves this problem and 'masks' the odious odours that emanate from our bodies and theirs.

Another benefit of smoking is that it destroys your taste buds and this makes food in unusual countries much more palatable. Furthermore, smoking is socially acceptable in these countries and you will become accepted as 'one of us' if you smoke.

Additionally, cigarettes can normally be used in place of currency in many unusual countries. You can tip young lads with cigarettes or bribe your way through customs with a twenty-pack of the best.

If you are a man then young women in unusual countries will be especially attracted to you if you smoke. They will think you're 'real macho' and you will remind them of Humphrey Bogart and the film they saw on TV last night.

Woe betide me for challenging these sacred anti smoking conventions but I think I have done enough in the above paragraphs to convince you of the merits of smoking in unusual countries. But don't do it back home because you might get caught!

Tip For Your Trip

Purchase ten duty free packs of cigarettes at the airport and carry these with you in a bright yellow carrier bag. Be generous in the way you smoke them.

42 POLLUTION

Politicians in unusual countries are not yet into this 'New Age' fad of environmentalism. They tend to have more important things on their minds like establishing billionaire bolt-holes in Europe.

Citizens of these countries are also more interested in eking out a living rather than keeping their air clean. For people who can only just afford a rusting clapped out motor car it is a bit much if the government requires them to make it environmentally friendly by restricting emissions.

The politicians of these countries are also in the pockets of the large Western companies that have invested significantly in heavy industry with its resultant major pollution. To clean up these industries would cost billions, which would be better used building bolt-holes for politicians and local industrialists in Europe. The additional billions would also price the country's products out of the reach of the global market and create even more unemployment.

Forest fires, traffic pollution and emissions from heavy industry are the norm for unusual countries; you will have to cough and splutter your way around them to get anywhere. Your eyes will also smart from the acid that is undoubtedly in the atmosphere.

In the capital cities of unusual countries you will never see a clean fresh river. Most of them contain filthy brown water that consists totally of chemical effluence that destroys all surrounding vegetation. Only human beings are resilient enough to live alongside such stagnant rivers. There is no greenery at all.

In some of these dreadful industrialised cities there are vast complexes of tall factory chimneys puffing out continuous streams of acrid yellow, sulphurous smoke, which destroys the environment. There is no green vegetation on which to rest a weary eye; instead you can see millions of tree skeletons on surrounding mountainsides. Theses are cities where the death rate from bronchial and respiratory diseases is exceptionally high, as are levels of cancer, still births and deformed babies.

Tip For Your Trip

If you suffer from asthma or any related problem it is best not to visit the capitals of most unusual countries. However, if you have to visit one of these countries take with you a breathing mask and a good supply of inhalers and antihistamines.

43 STOMACH AILMENTS

Every single person except one who has ventured outside their home country to visit an unusual country will have experienced a stomach disorder.

An important piece of advice is that whilst travelling to unusual countries you must not eat or drink anything. Should you give in to this temptation then the following precautions are mandatory. You must....

(a) .... avoid ice in cold drinks (thus making them warm)

(b) .... avoid salad foods (washed in filthy water)

(c) .... avoid sea foods (grown in filthy water)

(d) .... avoid undercooked meats (growing bacteria)

(e) .... avoid cooked meats (coated in bacteria)

(e) .... avoid fresh fruit (handled by dirty hands)

However, there is one antidote to stomach problems that I learnt about from one experienced traveller. He avoided every type of stomach disorder despite travelling to the extremities of the world over a period of twenty-five years.

He sold tractors for a living. This meant he had to visit people who lived in deserts, in jungles, in the bush, on the tops of mountains, in earthquake zones or in rain forests. He never stopped travelling and loved to mix with local people to whom of course he was trying to sell tractors.

He told me that before he ate a meal with these people he would always drink a large glass of neat whisky. This he assured me lined his stomach and killed off any germs that dared venture there.

After twenty five years of having no stomach disorders he went for a regular annual medical check up. The doctor told him he had cirrhosis of the liver and advised him to cut out alcohol. The poor man left the doctor feeling much worse than when he had gone in. Fearing death he gave up booze immediately.

On his very next trip to an unusual country he abstained from whisky. He contracted typhoid and died within three weeks.

Tip For Your Trip

Prior to taking off, visit the duty free shop at your friendly airport and purchase six litres of whisky to carry with you on your travels and to consume before eating (should you insist on eating).

44 DOCTORS

It is best not to get ill in unusual countries. If you do, self-healing is recommended. For this, take a wide range of medicines with you (see MEDICAL SUPPLIES).

Most doctors who are born in unusual countries are financially motivated. This means they do not work in unusual countries but practise in Europe or the USA. These are the best ones. The ones who do not make the grade tend to remain behind and will take great delight in practising on you, mainly because they can charge your insurance company a lot of money.

There is a saying in some parts of the world that people in the medical profession will "chop off your hand to sow up your finger." It is not because they are incompetent (they are) but because they make more money this way. Therefore they will be overcautious, over-diagnose, over-prescribe and generally demand twice as many consultations as necessary to boost their fee income.

The cost-effective solution is not to see a doctor at all. The real experts who can give you accurate advice are the pharmacists who you would have to go and see anyway. They know what's what and they will know precisely what drugs to give you to get you better. And they will sell them to you too. None of this nonsense with prescriptions that you have back home. If you have an infection and need some antibiotics don't see a doctor, see a pharmacist. You get better much more quickly that way.

As usual I exaggerate and to be fair there are one or two good doctors around in unusual countries. The way to find them is to use the 'network'. Basically this means asking around for a doctor who is recommended. Regrettably, you will find that everyone knows about these excellent doctors and therefore they will be much too busy to see you, unless you have a friend of a friend who is a friend of theirs and to whom the doctor owes a favour. In which case they might squeeze you into their already cram packed schedule. But still expect to wait.

Tip For Your Trip

Do not get ill abroad.

45 DYING

Warning: be careful how you die!

I wrote this section in the sweltering heat of a hotel bedroom in an unusual country. The air-conditioning was on but hardly coped with the heat. I waited for my driver to collect me (this took a long time) and I read a local newspaper. This was the headline (honestly!) and the news item:

HE WASN'T DEAD

Family claims man was alive when he was put in a mortuary freezer.

"The alleged freezing to death of a 43 year old businessman at the Police Hospital mortuary has generated a serious conflict.

"The deceased who was said to have been taken ill suddenly and fallen into a coma was sent to the Police Hospital mortuary for preservation without first being taken to see a medical officer.

"Apparently having been put in the freezer he emerged from his coma and struggled to get out. He then died properly."

There are many morals to this story; the main one being to avoid falling into a coma in an unusual country. If you do collapse, or faint, it is important to convince people that you are not dead.

One way of doing this is always to have a personal doctor accompany you on a trip. If the doctor himself collapses, or faints, or goes into a coma and you yourself are not a medical expert you now know what to do. You put the doctor into a mortuary freezer and see if he wakes up. This is the second lesson from the above true story.

Tip For Your Trip

Keep in your left hand upper pocket (from which muggers normally steal your money) a laminated photocopy of this page. This will alert your rescuers to the possibility that you might not be dead.

CHAPTER 4 HOTELS IN UNUSUAL COUNTRIES

In unusual countries people spend a lot of time sleeping. You will be one of them. The rigours of the travel and the terrain mean that you will be permanently tired and most of the time crave a decent bed. They can occasionally be found but you have to search for them.

Summarily when you seek accommodation in an unusual country you will have three choices:

(i) Shack up with a local in a local shack. This costs virtually nothing albeit there will be no amenities such as electricity, running water and flushing toilets. You will have to improvise like the locals do every day. Furthermore, you will have to sleep on a dirty old mattress on the floor alongside the rest of the family (much like sardines in a can).

(ii) Stay with a rich friend who has a colonial villa on the outskirts of town. This will also cost you virtually nothing albeit you'll have to put up with all your rich friend's stories, his modern amenities (which don't always work – such as mains electricity) and his servants (who also rarely work – spending much of their time, as you want to, sleeping).

(iii) Finally you can stay in a modern hotel, that's if you can find one. Generally these are expensive and not up to the standards you would normally expect.

In this chapter you will be given some expert guidance on the latter subject of hotels.

46 MODERN HOTELS

In many unusual countries modern civilisation is vested in only four types of buildings:

(a) The president's palace
(b) The local convention centre (conference centre, opera house, art gallery and museum all in one)
(c) Colonial villas for the rich
(d) Only one modern hotel

These hotels are, to be polite, a 'rip-off'. They will only allow you to pay in dollars or some other hard currency (but definitely not local currency) and the amount you pay for one night's stay is equivalent to two year's salary for a local executive. In these hotels the price of a soft drink will be ten times what you pay at the grubby little store around the corner.

Other features of these modern hotels are as follows:

(a) Excessive presence of security guards (to prevent locals coming in to use the toilets)
(b) Long queues at reception to check-in
(c) Even longer queues at reception to check-out
(d) Incredibly unfriendly staff (despite the high rate of unemployment and deprivation outside in the streets of the city)
(e) Swimming pools that look beautiful but are an instant source of eye infections, ear infections, stomach problems, impetigo, athlete's foot, boils, swellings and other mild ailments that can prove quite troublesome
(f) The slowest room service you will ever encounter
(g) The slowest restaurant service you will ever encounter
(h) Showers that don't work properly
(i) No trouser press
(j) Gorgeous prostitutes in the lobby after 8:00 pm (the security guards receive a commission)
(k) If you are a man, gorgeous prostitutes who knock at your bedroom door after 10:00 pm (they pay the concierge to inform them in which rooms single men are staying)
(l) Noise at night (from various sources, for example: prostitutes

at work, the sound of gunshots outside, the occasional explosion far away, the incessant wailing of sirens in the streets below, the barking of dogs, the wailing of certain demented people, the television from the room next door (the only one that works in the hotel))

(m) A customer comments card welcoming your feedback about your stay and promising to deliver the very best service anywhere

(n) A general manager who is never available except to meet VIPs and who does not tolerate complaints. "You have to understand that you're not back home now! Things are different here!"

These are of course the good hotels. There will be a number of other hotels which are not modern and are far better suited to the locals who can afford to stay in them. These are normally shacks and you are welcome to try them. I haven't.

Tips For Your Trip

As with many hotels in the UK it is wise to expect the worst. Then if your luck is in you might just be pleasantly surprised.

47 STRANGE TOILETS Part 2

You will not want to stay in a hotel room without a toilet, or, as I had to recently, in a hotel room where the toilet was a cubicle in the yard outside.

In fact, this is a very important consideration when visiting any unusual country. Before you depart you will need to undertake some research on toilets. If you are unfamiliar with the hotel that you are booked into, I suggest you make an international call and interrogate the person the other end about the quality of the toilets. This can be frustrating, of course, as it is unlikely anyone will answer your call and if they do they won't have the faintest idea what you are talking about. However, it is wise to persevere. You will need to explain to the local hotel switchboard operator in words of one syllable that you are used to the good things in life and want a modern toilet with a nice uncracked porcelain bowl and a spotlessly clean folding seat. Once they understand you will receive categorical assurance that each room has such a toilet.

True to their word you will actually find this to be the case on arrival. It will therefore be with some relief that you sit on the pan and reflect how things are not as bad in this hotel as you thought they might be. This is when you will notice a cockroach scurrying across the floor into a crack beneath the shower. When you lift your bum from the seat you will find the low quality lightweight plastic seat will stick to it and follow your bum around the room. This is because the seat has not been secured properly to the bowl.

What is worse, the flushing mechanism will not work properly. Sometimes, no matter how many times you yank the handle, water will not come out. Other times it will only be a trickle. In the slightly better hotels you can just about manage, with perseverance, to flush away most of what you want. But then you will have to wait for two hours whilst the cistern refills. This can be embarrassing if you are sharing a room with your beloved and on your first attempt you only flush away fifty-per-cent of your deposit.

There are some countries where it is illegal to flush toilet paper down the toilet. This is because when they built the sewage system none of the locals used toilet paper – and therefore to economise they only installed sewage pipes with narrow apertures – the sort that easily get blocked with paper. In these toilets a plastic basket is conveniently provided alongside the toilet bowl in which to put the paper with which you wipe your bum. I must admit you get used to this type of thing.

One final point. In your hotel toilet there will only be one small roll of toilet paper. By the third visit to the toilet all the paper will have gone. It is wise to be prepared for this.

Tip For Your Trip

Before departing buy a large 6 pack of luxury toilet tissue. Take this with you on your trip. It would also be useful to take a bucket with you for flushing the toilet. Furthermore undertake 'toilet research' before departing.

48 LIFTS (ELEVATORS)

Experienced travellers will know that power cuts are frequent in many unusual countries and can sometimes last three days. This is unfortunate if you get stuck in a lift.

Furthermore, lifts are not always well serviced in unusual countries, mainly because of a shortage of service engineers, a shortage of spare parts and a shortage of money. This means they can go wrong frequently.

Often these lifts are smelly with very poor lighting. When they do move they ascend at an alarming slow rate, making lots of creaking noises and appear to struggle to reach the floor you want. Conversely, they descend at an alarming speed giving the impression they have no brakes and will smash you to smithereens in the basement below.

If you do get stuck in a lift there is no way out. When there is a power cut the alarm bell will not work (you will not be able to see the red button on the panel because it will be pitch black inside the lift). Furthermore, they will have to fly in an engineer from the 'Regional Service Centre' to release you and this can take days.

In other words, it is best not to use lifts in unusual countries because there is a high probability that you will experience some sort of failure or deficiency leaving you with a psychiatric disorder.

The preferred route is to use the backstairs, even if this means walking up fourteen floors. You will still experience problems as firstly you will have difficulty in finding the stairs and when you do you find them in an even worse state than the lifts. Besides the smell, litter, excrement and urine stains you will come across dead rats, rotting hamburgers that date back ten years when the building was first built and the occasional dead human body (I am of course exaggerating just a little, but it has been known).

When you reach the fourteenth floor in the sweltering heat you will find that the door to the hotel floor you wanted is locked and that you have to go all the way down again to fetch a key.

These problems always happen to visitors and never to locals who will only laugh at your predicament. It is their way of telling you that you bring bad 'feng shui' to their hotel.

Tip For Your Trip

Do not use lifts (elevators) in unusual countries. If you insist, ensure you always step into a lift with the lady (or man) of your dreams.

49 POWER FAILURES

Power failures happen daily in some unusual countries – or to be exact nightly. On one particular occasion my room was a small wooden bungalow in the grounds of the hotel. It was late at night and as I strolled back to my room the heavens suddenly opened and the monsoon rains came down. Just like that! There was no warning. Then all the lights went out including the lamps illuminating the path I was on. It was pitch back, I could not see where I was going and the downpour was immense. I kept on stumbling off the path and into bushes (and I had not even been drinking alcohol!). I expected a tiger to jump out on me.

With some relief I turned to see some lights come on behind me. Apparently, the main hotel building had an emergency generator - but only with enough power for the reception area. I found my way back and bumped into the duty manager who told me the power cut could last anything from three hours to three days. I was desperately tired and didn't fancy sleeping on the bench in reception. The manager collared a porter, asked him to fetch an umbrella a torch and guide me back to my room.

The porter led me into my room and let me in. He refused to lend me his torch (apparently there was only one in the hotel) and then left me to my own devices in my pitch black room. I could not see anything!

I groped my way around and flopped on to the bed. It was so dark I couldn't even find my way to the bathroom. I literally felt as if I was blindfolded.

Then at four o'clock in the morning, when I was deep in sleep in my wet clothes on top of the bed, all the lights came on, the radio alarm screamed, the air-conditioning noisily resurrected itself and suddenly I was awake, having flopped out at midnight. Such are the adventures you can have in unusual countries.

Tip For Your Trip

Always carry a small pocket torch in your pocket. You never know when it is going to come in useful.

As a backup you might also consider carrying a candle, a candlestick holder and a box of matches.

50 BEDROOM LIGHTS

This is a typical problem: trying to work out how to turn the lights on and off in your hotel bedroom.

In some hotel rooms the lighting circuits and switches will be so complicated that it will take you at least half-an-hour trying to work out how to turn them on. And then, having discovered this you will need another hour trying to work out how to turn them off.

In one hotel room I stayed in there were three lamps above my bed, two further wall lights, two upright lamp standards, plus a light in the corridor leading to the toilet, plus the light in the toilet. That was nine lights in total.

The trouble was there were fifteen switches in the room. A certain combination of switches would turn on the lamps above my bed, but there was no way I could get the two upright lamp standards to throw some light on the room. Was there something wrong with the bulbs?

I poked around the lamp standards themselves and could see no on-off switch. I followed the cables all the way to the wall socket and still couldn't find any switch.

I tried every combination of switches possible and I still couldn't switch on the lamp standards. In the process I accidentally turned on the television (which I couldn't get to work previously because I didn't know I had to turn it on from a wall switch).

I finally succeeded in getting the two lamp standards to come on. I forgot which combination of switches I used but at least I was able to read my book with a reasonable degree of 40w light. I decided to leave all the lights on whilst I went down for dinner.

On returning and before going to bed I tried to turn off the lights. I succeeded except for the lamp standards. I had to go through the whole convoluted discovery process again.

Tip For Your Trip

Take with you a graph book, a black and a red pen, a ruler and then prepare a map linking the various light switches in your room to the various lights.

51 TELEPHONES

Some unusual countries are getting better at this. But not many. Do not assume that your cellphone will be able to pick up a signal in a remote region, even if you have international roaming.

It might still be necessary to use the hotel's landline should you wish to ring your partner to advise him or her of your safe arrival.

I would normally allow an extra day for this. If you want some practice in real frustration trying ringing home from an unusual country. In the bad old days you would have to book your call at a specified time. Now they don't bother because you can never get a line.

Rest assured, or lack of rest assured, you will eventually get through. However, it will never be the first time. You will hear on the line every conceivable clicking noise you have ever heard in your life.

There have been miraculous moments when I have thought I have got through to my beloved only to hear her voice fade further and further into the distance until it became the normal silence we experience at home.

I have tried different types of chargecards, different calling routines, I have tried everything but if the satellites in the heavens are against you then even praying will do no good.

These tribulations do not only relate to international calls. Try ringing a local number and you will always find it engaged - this is because most local people spend all their lives on the telephone. When someone answers it is often a servant who doesn't speak English, doesn't know what you are talking about, squawks a few strange words at you and then puts the phone down.

It is worth also checking the cost before making a call. Some hotels charge an extortionate amount – as do some cell phone service providers. Furthermore, some hotels even charge you for failed calls.

Tip For Your Trip

Allow an extra three days on your trip to make telephone calls.

52 WAKE-UP CALLS

I recently did a study of wake-up calls in hotels I had been staying at in unusual countries. The results are as follows:

Percentage Of Requested Hotel Wake-up Calls	
46.4 %	fail to happen
43.6 %	are up to half an hour late (never half an hour early)
10 %	are within +/- five minutes of the desired time
0 %	(none) are ever on time (i.e. +/- one minute)

Following many complaints from many travellers most hotels now put alarm radios into your room thus allowing you to take complete responsibility for your own wake-up call. However, this is less than ideal. You can spend up to an hour before going to bed trying to work out how these alarm radios work (there are of course no instructions available). Frequently they have red digital numbers or funny letters like 'r' or 'e' flashing at you. Whatever you do you will be unable to stop these red lights flashing.

Having given up you will then be woken in the middle of the night with a terrible ear-shattering din from the radio alarm, having inadvertently set the alarm for the wrong time. You will then spend ten minutes trying to work out how to turn on the lights (see earlier section on LIGHTS) and then a further ten minutes trying to work how to turn off the alarm.

Even if you do not tamper with your bedside radio alarm it will still go off in the middle of the night because the previous incumbent in your bed had a 4:00 am departure from your hotel to catch a flight – and nobody bothered to reset the alarm.

It must be recognised that nothing in unusual countries is easy.

Tip For Your Trip

If you have an early start in the morning it is wise to take at least three alarm clocks with you. The first you will forget to set to local time and will thus go off at the wrong time. The second will have a flat battery. The third will work and will wake you up in time…

53 KEEPING VALUABLES SAFE

I am frequently told by the so-called experts never to leave anything of value around in hotel rooms and to always use safety deposit boxes available either in your wardrobe or reception. I never bother because I always forget the combination codes necessary to open these things and furthermore, the safes are never big enough for my laptop.

To be honest in twenty years of travelling around the world and staying in some very strange hotels I have never had a problem. I do of course apply a modicum of limited common sense. I therefore do not leave out hundreds of dollars for all to see, nor do I leave my credit cards around or my camera or my precious laptop computer. I normally lock all these away in my case.

I also take some additional positive steps to ensure my valuables are safe. I always make friends with the housekeeping staff; especially the people who clean my room and make my bed. I go out of my way to chat, to compliment them on the excellent job they are doing and to find out about their own personal circumstances.

Let's take for example Faustina, a lovely lady I encountered a couple of years ago. She had been working at the hotel for over ten years. She was very happy. She was a single mum with three children, her 'man' having left her for a younger woman twelve years ago. Her mother, her aunt and three nieces also lived with her. They all lived in one room. She was the only one working and earned $US14 for working six days a week, cleaning twenty hotel rooms every day. She seemed quite happy with that. It kept the whole family in food, and just about paid the rent, plus the illegal supply of electricity from the shanty town mafia.

To keep her on my side I always asked Faustina to do something extra for me, like provide me with an additional bar of soap or provide more towels. Faustina took delight in helping me in this way and I took delight in giving her little presents in recognition of her extra efforts, for example a couple of dollars to buy something for the kids. Whilst at the hotel, Faustina became my best friend. Every morning she waited by the housekeeping trolley looking out for me after breakfast, hoping to catch my eye, have a friendly word and perhaps do something extra for me.

As a result I never had a problem with things disappearing from my room. It was as simple as that. Treat people honestly, fairly and with dignity and they will do the same for you.

Tip For Your Trip

Always be friendly to hotel staff and be exceptionally generous with your gifts to them. To achieve this effect take with you two hundred dollars to give away.

54 TROUSER PRESS

For reasons which I will not go into it is wise for women to wear trousers when visiting unusual countries. At least this puts them on a par with men when it comes to fulfilling such essential needs as getting trousers pressed.

Most sensible travellers wear trousers on aeroplanes and have at least one spare pair packed in their luggage. When you arrive at your destination you will find both pairs horribly creased.

In nine out of ten unusual countries there will be no trouser press in your hotel bedroom. On the tenth occasion there will be one but it will not work.

Occasionally you will find an iron and ironing board in your room. Under no circumstances should these be used. They are absolutely deadly and have been known to electrocute guests, burn them dreadfully and (what is worse) destroy their trousers.

The only solution is to persuade a member of hotel staff to press your trousers for you. This can be very difficult. Most modern hotels have a laundry service (see next section) which only operates from 8:00 a.m. in the morning until 6:00 p.m. in the evening. Invariably you will arrive at your hotel outside these times but, even so, will be desperate to have your trousers pressed ready for that important dinner engagement with your tour guide.

You will therefore have to bribe a volunteer from hotel staff to press your trousers for you. This can take anything up to four hours as normally hotel staff will not understand your precise requirements. On one occasion when my trousers did not return, the member of staff had assumed that as I had no cash on me I was giving them to him in lieu of a tip. On another occasion a member of staff kept my trousers because he thought I had said "present" when I had actually said "pressing".

My late grandfather, who was in the army, advised me that he used to press his uniform by laying it out under his bed (they had hard mattresses in the army). I tried this once in an unusual country and the following morning found the trousers all stained (from god knows what) as well as full of little holes from where the bed bugs had been hard at work.

Tip For Your Trip

If you want to look smart and impress people every evening always take with you a Corby trouser press (with a multi-adaptor plug).

55 LAUNDRY

Laundry services in unusual countries can be a nightmare. In fact, I have so many anecdotes on laundries that I am tempted to write a whole book on the subject.

I cannot think of a single occasion when the laundry service in a hotel in an unusual country worked perfectly.

In some countries it is so incredibly hot and humid that you are just forced to wear three shirts a day (not at the same time I should add). You therefore have no option but to use the laundry service offered by the hotel. The following research data (compiled by myself) reveals what can happen to your laundry in unusual countries:

(i) Your laundry is not returned and the hotel denies it had it in the first place

(ii) Someone else's laundry is returned

(iii) Your shirts are returned on hangers when you wanted it folded – or vice versa

(iv) Your laundry is returned starched when you wanted them unstarched – or vice versa

(v) Your laundry is returned in boxes that are sealed with vicious staples so that you cut your fingers and tear your clothes in opening them up

(vi) Your laundry is returned in heat-sealed plastic and is impossible to open

(vii) Only part of your laundry is returned

(viii) Your laundry is returned only after you have spent the whole evening making innumerable telephone calls chasing it and spoken to every single person in the hotel

(ix) Your laundry is returned after you check-out

(x) Your laundry is returned wet

(xi) Your laundry is returned damaged

(xii) Your laundry is waiting to be collected at the concierge whilst you are waiting for it to be delivered

(xiii) You ring laundry at 7:30 a.m. in the morning and ask them to collect your laundry. You return at 7:30 p.m. in the evening to find it is still there

(xiv) Your laundry is available for sale at the local street market

You may have wondered why really rich people have their own personal valets to accompany them on trips. Now you know why.

Tip For Your Trip

Take with you on your trip two large boxes of detergent and one large bottle of fabric conditioner (never available in unusual countries) for washing your own clothes together with a hair-drier for drying them.

Alternatively hire a personal valet to accompany you on your trip.

56 COAT HANGERS

Coat hangers, or the absence of them, can prove to be a particular nuisance in unusual countries, especially if you have some important events to attend.

It is rare that I find more than four coat hangers in a closet or wardrobe and I normally need six. Often the coat hangers provided are bent bits of wire or broken bits of plastic.

On one occasion I only found one coat hanger and rang down to reception to request more. I was instructed to ring housekeeping. I did so and nobody answered. So I rang reception again only to be informed that housekeeping finished at 6:00 pm and this was 6:05 pm. It took me twenty-four hours to get a new supply of coat hangers.

On another occasion I ventured out to the local street market to purchase twenty plastic coat hangers for a dollar. I was then able to hang up my clothes and still had ten spare. I foolishly left these hanging with no clothes on. That evening when I returned I found my spare coat hangers had disappeared. No doubt they were back on sale in the market.

Tip For Your Trip

Take with you on your trip at least ten plastic coat hangers and a long chain to secure them to the rusting chrome rail in your hotel room wardrobe.

57 SHOELACES

This is the reality of travel. You don't sleep too well and then wake up jet-lagged feeling dreadful. Desperate for sleep, you put off getting out of bed until the last minute. You struggle with a shower that has yet to find its vocation in life. You quickly shave (if you are a man and possibly if you are a woman) and cut yourself in the process.

You dress, put on your shoes and then it happens. Your shoelace breaks.

It is one of the most perverse irritations that happens in life but shoelaces always break at the most awkward times when you are in a rush and when you want to look smart.

I normally go into panic mode when this happens. I angrily extract the broken lace out of the shoe and attempt to recycle the shortened lace through the eyelets. To do this I need my spectacles - but I cannot find them. What did I do with my glasses last night? Having found them I then discover that there is not enough lace to go through the five pairs of eyelets, so I have to forgo one pair of eyelets and hope no one notices.

A better idea suddenly springs to mind. I call down to reception and ask them whether they have any shoelaces. They do not understand. They have never heard of shoelaces. I then hobble down to reception in shoes which have not been tied in order to demonstrate the problem. I should have known anyway that they would not have shoelaces. The best answer you can expect is "Try the gift shop". But the gift shop does not open for another hour and a half.

By this time I am too late for breakfast as the tour bus is due to leave in ten minutes. Without food I am grumpy all morning. It is this sort of thing that causes divorces.

All for a pair of shoelaces.

Tip For Your Trip

It is essential that you have at least six assorted pairs of shoelaces packed during travels.

58 REPAIRS

Recently I was assigned a hotel room in which the air-conditioning would not work. It just would not come on and I was baking. I rang reception and after waiting forty-five minutes they sent an engineer (or handyman to be exact). Five hours later and five visits later he still had not got the air-conditioning to work. Of course they had no spare room to which to move me.

This about sums up the approach to repairs in unusual countries. You can put it down to a lack of training or service orientation but when something goes wrong in an unusual country you are going to have a huge problem.

Often the problem relates to a lack of spare parts which have to be imported at horrendous cost. Their solution is either to use cannibalised spare parts or imitation 'pirated' spare parts. This is why your air-conditioning or television will not work, they have probably cannibalised it to supply spare parts to another defective unit. It is a vicious circle.

Many things you will be unable to get repaired, like your camera, your cellphone and your hearing-aid. You will find many people who volunteer to try but most of them are of dubious skill and experience.

If you are a millionaire the solution is simple. You replace the broken-down equipment with new. When you do this miracles will happen. A local will buy your old broken down equipment at a fraudulently low price. You will then discover it for sale in a shop or salesroom the next day. It will of course now be working perfectly. This is the selfsame equipment that they had previously been unrepairable.

The very worst problem is when the battery of your heart pacemaker runs out. The number of people who have died in unusual countries because of this is immeasurable.

Tip For Your Trip

As a contingency you would be well-advised to take a tool kit with you when visiting an unusual country. This should include the following:

(i)   a Swiss army penknife

(ii)   a hammer

(iii) a long screwdriver

(iv)   a pack of fuses

(v)   a variety of fuse wires

(vi)   ordinary wire

(vii) string and a good selection of screws and cable clips

(vii) a spare battery for your pacemaker

You will then be in the perfect position to tackle defective air-conditioning units and other equipment that does not work in your hotel room or in your body.

59 HOTEL CUSTOMER SERVICE

Many readers of this learned guide will have attended more customer service training courses than they can bear to think about.

No wonder so many people are now choosing to visit unusual countries "I am sorry boss, but that date you gave me for the customer service training course is the date of my holiday in an unusual country." Anything to get out of customer service training!

Being experts in customer service most readers will be staggered to find that the concept is unheard of in unusual countries and no one, literally no one, puts into practice all those important techniques taught on training courses (just like you never put them into practice yourself).

At best you will find a customer comment card in your hotel bedroom. It will be dog-eared as no customer ever bothers to fill it in – for the simple reason that they know that no one from the hotel will ever read such things let alone do anything about the comments.

On arrival at the hotel you will not even receive a smile. You will meet miserable staff at reception who keep their eyes down and who make you wait for ages as they try to find your reservation and then inform you your room is not ready. The person who takes your luggage to the room will provide the best service in the hotel. He will smile at you and ask you about your flight. This is because he expects a nice big tip. It is the best paid job in the hotel and there is a great demand for them.

When you go down to the restaurant for dinner or breakfast you will be totally ignored. The waiters and waitresses will stand around chatting amongst themselves – just like back in the UK. You will not exist in their eyes. To order a simple cup of tea will prove a great ordeal.

The only people who will be friendly in the hotel are those who can reasonably expect a tip. As it is impossible to tip every single hotel employee you can generally expect to receive dreadful customer service.

Some hotels do add a service charge to your bill. However, this makes no difference as the staff never receive this money. It goes to management.

Tip For Your Trip

Be patient, be tolerant and lower your expectations. If you think customer service is bad in the UK then visit an unusual country.

60 COMPLAINING

The word 'complaint' does not exist in the local languages of most unusual countries. Therefore, local people have no concept at all of what complaining is about.

Whatever goes wrong it is best not to complain for this will only make matters worse. You might have years of practice back home but it will be naiveté of the highest order to complain and assume the problem will be rectified as a result.

The best that can happen when you complain is that they will smile warmly at you, agree completely with what you say, try to charm you and then do nothing about your complaint – ever.

More often than not when you complain you will be completely ignored. The person to whom you are complaining will pretend not to understand what you are saying and seize the first opportunity to change the subject.

Should you ask to see the manager to complain you will normally find that he is not available. If you decide to wait until he is available you will discover that he will continue to be unavailable until you have gone. If you do catch him walking past and confront him he will listen politely before calling over the nearest employee and bollocking him in front of everyone. You will be hated for this.

The worst that can happen is that the person to whom you are complaining takes things personally and starts losing his temper, blaming you for everything, telling you it's your fault the television is not working, that the food was cold, and that the luggage was lost. Arms will start flailing and you will be made to feel very bad.

Tip For Your Trip

If you do have a complaint the best thing is not to complain but to ask for a favour. This can work miracles because you are playing on the individual's self-esteem and feelings of importance. Favours imply generous tips.

It's a lesson my grandfather taught me years ago, "It's not 'what' you say, it's 'how' you say it." It's a lesson that is certainly applicable in unusual countries.

The other option of course is not to complain at all, to turn the other cheek and demonstrate your excessive powers of tolerance.

61 THINGS THAT DON'T WORK

Nothing works properly in unusual countries. Full stop. People don't even work properly as we know it.

To illustrate this fundamental point let's take hotel bedrooms. Various points have already been covered in this comprehensive guide but it's important that we now include a few others.

In your hotel bedroom it will not be easy to pull out the drawers (if at all) to stow away your clothes. These drawers will be made of heavy wood without any runners at all. The doors to the toilet and the wardrobe (closet) will not shut properly and many lights will not function.

It is rare (even back home) to find a shower that works properly. You will find many irregularities about showers in unusual countries.

Here are some:

(a) You cannot fathom how to start the shower

(b) When eventually opened only a trickle of water comes out

(c) The water is freezing even when the control is turned to red hot

(d) The water is boiling even when the control is turned to cold

(e) The water splashes everywhere except on you

(f) When you step out afterwards the water from the shower will not drain away and will remain as a stagnating puddle for a couple of days

There will be no bath in the room and if there is you will not want to use it.

The air-conditioning will either be too noisy or too cold.

The bed will creak and so will the floorboards. This is great as a form of contraception but irritating when you were hoping for an adventure holiday.

As mentioned previously toilets, if they are of the modern type, often do not flush properly and can take up to two hours for the cistern to refill.

The alarm clock, the radio and the television will rarely work and will come on at random times, normally in the middle of the night.

I have yet to find the perfect hotel room in an unusual country. In fact, it is rare that I find that anything works properly in an unusual country.

Tip For Your Trip

Never expect perfection in an unusual country.

62 BEACHES

Beaches have been grossly over-represented in the media. Every day we are bombarded with images of paradise ..and with white beaches, clear blue seas and beautiful palm trees. Our fantasies are created around these beaches.

When you arrive on one of these beaches the other side of the hotel compound this is what you will actually find:

(a) Assorted pedlars selling nasty trinkets, dodgy ice cream and warm beer

(b) Litter of every description including used condoms, syringes, broken glass, ring-pulls from empty cans, fag-ends and discarded pornographic magazines

(c) Dead animals including washed-up seagulls, the skeletons of fish and dogs partly eaten by sharks

(d) Dead jellyfish, live jellyfish (of the killer variety)

(e) Bits of wood (washed up)

(f) Bits of wood (upright) with bullet holes in

(g) Bits of wood (also upright) where the locals will tell you they hung and shot members of the government after the last coup d'etat

(h) Bits of rusty metal from discarded vehicles and other equipment

(i) Indescribably smelly rotting vegetation

(j) Seaweed

(k) Oil, tar and faeces of every description

As if this is not enough you will also find the deadly razor-fish and also the stone-fish. Shoals of these creatures swim around in shallow water and have a tendency to get stranded at low tide. They then hide in the sand waiting for the water to return. Whilst they idle their time away there is nothing they like to do more than strike down bathers who dare to walk over them. Unless you can get to a hospital within thirty minutes you will be dead.

The sea itself is no better. Whilst it looks idyllically blue from afar, on closer inspection you will find that it will be polluted with the sewage tipped overboard from the millionaires yacht anchored in the bay. It is therefore advisable to keep your mouth above

_r whilst swimming. A little way out you will be able to see the
casional shark basking in the sun. Watch out for stingrays too.

Occasionally you might even find a real human body (of the dead variety) floating in the sea.

When the wind gets up and waves appear on the sea there is a high risk that you will be deceived into thinking that these are like the civilised waves you find at home. In fact, the waves in unusual countries always have phenomenal undertows which will drag you under, hit your head on the sand and then sweep you out helplessly towards the horizon.

Overall, it is best to keep to the bacterially polluted swimming pool in your hotel and avoid the beach.

Tip For Your Trip

A heavy pair of sandals is recommended for beaches.

63 HOTEL BARS

Hotel bars in unusual countries are depressing places. Very little thought will have been given to their design and they tend to be cold, unwelcoming places with torn leather seating, anaemic lighting and grumpy bartenders.

Often you will find a television blaring (normally sport) in the background so it will be impossible to talk.

Few people will frequent these bars and often the air-conditioning will be turned on so high you will freeze to death.

The range of drinks available will be limited to one type of beer, two types of whisky and three types of soft drink (lemonade, orangeade and cola). Whatever the drink, it is guaranteed you will be overcharged.

With luck they will serve you nuts with your drinks.

The only women who frequent these establishments are hookers. They sit elegantly on high stools at the bar taking care to reveal seductive portions of their thighs whilst glancing at you every thirty seconds. They will pretend to sip their drinks and mime their conversation with the barman whilst concentrating their gaze on you. The more you try to avoid their eyes the more you will find yourself glancing at them. That is their trick.

It is very difficult to conduct a conversation in one of these bars let alone enjoy yourself, unless you find the prospect of becoming diseased, divorced and despairing enjoyable. Personally I, find such places depressing and prefer my own company and that of a good book in the privacy of my bedroom.

I have therefore learnt in my old age to avoid such bars and if I am to have a conversation with a friend I tend to use the reception area of the hotel, but even then you can be distracted by hookers and hawkers.

Most of my friends overseas tell me it is no fun getting drunk in an unusual country. That's why so many of them love to visit London. It's such a good place to get drunk.

Tip For Your Trip

Abstain from alcohol (except for medicinal purposes) when visiting an unusual country. If you insist on visiting bars then pack a nice thick woolly cardigan to prevent the air-conditioning from freezing you to death. It will also tend to stop the hookers staring at you.

64 THE INTERNET

It would be unfair for you to assume that unusual countries do not have computers and internet capability. They do.

However, the systems they use are the type that went out of date in the Victorian era in the UK. For example, many hotels do not even have a broadband facility but seem to rely on some old-fashioned technique where you have to dial a number to get connected to the internet. Younger readers will find this unbelievable, never having experienced incredibly slow wire connections with their time-consuming downloads.

Generally, hotels have the worst internet provision and you would be well advised to seek out and use an internet café in the capital city. These will prove much cheaper as your hotel will charge at least a dollar a minute for a service which can take a quarter of an hour to open one hotmail page. (If you complain they will blame hotmail for being very busy at this time of the day). Internet cafés by comparison only charge a dollar an hour.

Internet cafés are great places for meeting people and chatting away whilst you wait for your hotmail pages to open. The screens are so tightly packed together you can even read your neighbours email or watch them playing games on the screen. This is not the time to visit porn sites as you will definitely get arrested. What is worse (or even better) you might recognise the porn star as the person sitting next to you in the internet café.

Personally, I am very encouraged by the increasing use of the internet in unusual countries as it does stop wars.

Tip For Your Trip

Those of you visiting an unusual country for the purpose of an adventure holiday should completely forget about keeping in touch with your loved ones back home. You can waste a lot of time in internet cafés and, as a result, miss out on opportunities to discover the wonders of the unusual country you are in.

CHAPTER 5

TRAVELLING TO, FROM AND AROUND UNUSUAL COUNTRIES

Those of you who have experienced the teeming crowds at Heathrow airport on a Monday morning or the thirty miles of traffic jams along the M4 motorway late on a Friday afternoon will have had a glimpse of hell. Multiply the aggravation factor by ten and you will have some idea of what travelling to, from and around an unusual country is like.

It is not easy and that is a euphemism. In fact it's hell! You can be guaranteed that nothing from start to finish will go smoothly and you will be subjected to a travelling ordeal beyond the imagination of decent folks who expect things to go their way.

Personally I hate the travelling bit. When I get there and am settled in my cockroach infested hotel then I begin to enjoy myself because I do meet some fascinating people – no matter how incompetent they are. However the process of getting there, getting around and getting back can be far from pleasant – as you will find out in the following sections.

65 VISAS

It can be a rude awakening but you have to realise that most of the authorities in unusual countries don't want you there in the first place. Foreigners like you cause problems. To keep you out they have thousands of people who create complicated visa entry requirements and then ensure that the requirements are met, in triplicate.

This will of course also remind you of the UK and the British Home Office. They set the international benchmark for being difficult.

You should treat a trip to an unusual country like a major project, it's not like Europe where you can hop onto an aeroplane, fly a few hundred miles, flick a passport at an immigration officer and leisurely stroll into the country. Step one of the project of travelling to an unusual country is acquiring a visa.

First you will need at least five passport photos. These are relatively easy to obtain albeit most automatic photo machines (the types you get at Woolworths or at railway stations) only issue four at a time.

You will then need a visa application form. In theory these should be available from your local travel agency but they never are, especially for unusual countries. You will need to allow at least a week to obtain these forms from the embassy.

The more progressive unusual countries now allow you to download these forms from the internet.

Visa application forms have to be filled out in triplicate and tend to ask difficult questions such as "What is the maiden name of your mother?" or "Give the names of three referees in the country you are visiting".

If you plan to work in an unusual country your visa application will normally need to be accompanied by a letter of invitation from your sponsor. Faxes are unacceptable as the officials at the embassy like to see the colour of the ink on the letterhead. As mail does not work in these countries it is best to get these letters of invitation sent to you by courier. Allow three weeks and three further chasing faxes for this.

These unusual countries have realised that sticking fancy coloured visas into passports is a good way of making money. So they will charge you the earth for one. Even then they have a nice little scam by which errors will be made on your visa so that the officials can spot them and be bribed to let you in.

Normally, allow two weeks for your visa to be processed through the embassy. On no account visit the embassy yourself. You can waste days waiting there. Overall, from start to finish allow at least two months to obtain your visa. If you are travelling during this period it is wise to have a second passport. I do.

Some countries trick you another way. They do not insist on a pre-flight visa but will issue you one on arrival providing you join a long queue and pay a hefty sum of cash. Other countries demand payments when you leave the country.

Tip For Your Trip

A check-in lady once told me I would be amazed at the number of people who arrive for their flight having forgotten their passport. This might sound like teaching your grandmother to suck eggs, always ensure you have a valid passport and visa with you before you leave home for an unusual country.

66 AIRLINE SCHEDULES

The airline schedules to unusual countries are all the same. Basically they are as follows

Flight arrival at capital city airport, unusual country............midnight
Arrive at hotel down town ....3:00 am
(for which you will be charged a full night's stay).

On departure the reverse applies.
Flight departure from capital city airport, unusual country.......2:30 am
(having departed from your hotel down town at midnight. You will also be charged a full night's stay when leaving at midnight).

There are a few flights that are scheduled to leave before 10:30 pm in the evening. However, these are always delayed for four hours so it amounts to the same thing anyway.

When you fly in just before midnight, or take-off in the middle of the night you will often be given a guided air tour by the pilot of the local suburbs and shanty towns. If you have a window seat you will be able to see these quite vividly because the lights of the shacks below you will still be on. This is because the locals living near airports cannot sleep.

The reason people cannot sleep is because back in Europe people wish to sleep. So you are not allowed to land an aircraft or take-off during night time. This means that the arrival and departure of flights in unusual countries has to be delayed until the middle of the night so that they can depart and arrive during the civilised hours of 5:00 am to 11:00 pm in Europe. This enables Europeans living near airports to wake up naturally, have a leisurely shower, a mug of green tea, a bowl of Swiss muesli, a slice of organic toast and watch a little bit of breakfast television to see how their shares are doing before being afflicted with their first aircraft noise of the day. Europeans do not give a toss for the poor sleepless people living in tin huts just beyond the perimeter's edge of airports in unusual countries. Nor does anyone else for that matter.

Tip For Your Trip

Given these schedules it is always advisable to allow two extra days, one at each end of your trip, to recover from the ordeal of a sleepless night flight in a cramped backbreaking, neck-cricking aeroplane seat.

Alternatively, you could take a sleeping pill just as you get on the return flight.

67 BOARDING AEROPLANES

This is where all your training in jungle warfare comes into play. When boarding aeroplanes in unusual countries you just have to be ruthless.

First you will need to have your flight confirmed 72 hours before departure. This is difficult if you only arrived the day before. Furthermore, the airline phone numbers will always be engaged. It is best to get someone else who knows the ropes to confirm the flight for you (see section on TIPPING).

On arrival at the check-in there is a possibility they will have not heard of you, will not accept your ticket, will tell you the flight is overbooked and that they have no seat for you. To overcome this type of problem it is essential that you arrive at the airport early and be prepared to pull out your wallet to ease your passage (see section on BRIBING).

The boarding pass you eventually receive at check-in does not guarantee you a seat on the aeroplane. When the flight is overbooked the airline staff will frequently issue 110 boarding passes (say) for 97 seats on the aeroplane. Obtaining a seat is therefore on a first come first served basis. The passengers who don't get seats either stand (during the whole flight) or fight the crew and refuse to get off the plane. This can cause immense delays.

It is thus essential you get on the aeroplane first. To accomplish this wait by the gate and make sure you get on the first bus to arrive when the flight is eventually called. Once on the bus do not sit down but stand by the door (even if this blocks the entrance of others). Make sure you are the first to clamber up the stairs of the aircraft in order to obtain the pick of the seats, even if this means elbowing other people aside.

Airlines in unusual countries rarely allocate seats by seat row number. The best seats are aisle seats near the forward emergency exits. This will enable you to escape easily if the plane crashes. Normally there is insufficient overhead stowage space for all passengers. This is another reason for getting on the plane first, you can then commandeer as much stowage space as you need.

Once seated do not move on any account, even if a flight attendant asks you to. Pretend not to speak English if necessary.

If someone comes down the aisle and you don't like the look of them glare at this person so that they do not sit next to you. Also make sure you place your elbow on the armrest and keep it there for the whole flight when someone sits next to you. Once you take your elbow off you will never get the armrest back again.

I am afraid that when it comes to boarding aircraft charity, kindness, helpfulness and common courtesy go out of the window. If you want to get to your destination you should only think of 'number one'.

Tip For Your Trip

Study this page carefully before boarding an aircraft in an unusual country.

68 ARRIVING IN AN UNUSUAL COUNTRY

If you have never done so before, arriving in an unusual country can be quite traumatic. It is not as simple as showing your passport, collecting your luggage and then waving to your friendly tour representative who has come to meet you on the other side of the barrier.

It is a thousand times more complicated. First of all on descending from the aircraft you will have to fight to get on a cramped bus which will keep you waiting for twenty minutes to squeeze the last person (in a wheelchair) on. The bus will then drive you 120 metres across the tarmac (in order to keep bus drivers in jobs). You will then have to go through a health check, presenting your yellow card to prove that you have been inoculated (or is it vaccinated?) against hepatitis, typhoid, cholera and rabies. This will take another twenty minutes (the queues will always be long and there will always only be one official available). Next you will have to search for a pink form to declare how much currency you are bringing into the country. The longest wait will be to have your passport and visa checked. On one occasion in an unusual country I waited from midnight to 3:00 a.m. in the morning whilst the customs officer processed each person in the queue fifteen minutes at a time.

There will then be a long wait for your luggage in the arrivals area. Here the toilets will be filthy and there will be no seats. There will be more porters than passengers and each porter will steer a trolley towards you trying to secure your business.

Having waited a further half an hour, your bags will occasionally arrive. You will then have to queue a further half an hour to go through customs where the customs officer will meticulously go through your tightly packed case to make sure you are not hiding contraband. As mentioned in the section on BRIBERY there are ways of avoiding this bit.

On emerging from the airport with a porter in tow you will find a thousand faces staring at you as if you were a pop star coming on stage. Each will be waving a piece of paper and you will have to inspect each one in a vain attempt to find one with your name on it. The law of perversity dictates that your name is not there and that your tour representative or host, who has come all the way to meet you, is not present at the correct time.

Your porter will desert you as soon as you emerge into the crowd whereupon one hundred touts will descend upon you trying to persuade you to use their taxi. They will grab your trolley and start wheeling it away.

Out of the blue, when you are at the final point of desperation your tour representative will emerge and rescue you. Welcome to an unusual country.

Tip For Your Trip

Ensure you have the telephone numbers of everyone, including your tour representative, your hotel and reputable local taxi firms.

69 DEPARTING FROM AN UNUSUAL COUNTRY

There is a certain bravado amongst local people who are meant to be looking after you in an unusual country.

"What time is your flight back?" They will ask.

"Ten o'clock this evening." you will lie, knowing it's ten thirty.

"I reckon if you leave at nine o'clock you will have plenty of time," your host will tell you, "I'll pick you up for dinner at eight and take you on to the airport afterwards."

Do not fall for this trap, especially if there are only two flights a week to your home country. Tell them you want to get to the airport early and do some duty free shopping or that you want to ring your partner from the airport. Make any excuse but do not allow your host to control your journey back to the airport. If you do arrive early it's much better to sit back and relax with a drink, reading a good book than be sitting in a traffic jam and fretting whether or not you are going to miss the flight.

From my experience this is how I normally plan for a journey back to the airport for a 10:30 pm flight, even when I suspect it's going to depart four hours late.

6:00 p.m.	Call the concierge from your room to have your cases collected. Wait half an hour.
6:30 pm	Porter arrives to collect cases. Accompany him to reception to check out. Spend half an hour arguing with cashier over mistakes in bill.
7:00 pm	Wait for the driver who was supposed to collect you at 7:00 pm.
7:15 pm	Depart from the hotel.
7:30 pm	Sit in first traffic jam for half an hour.
8:00 pm	Sit in second traffic jam for half an hour.
8:30 p.m.	Arrive at airport.
	Stand in a scrummage for twenty minutes to get through security before they even let you into the departures area.

8:50 pm	Stand in a scrummage for another twenty minutes to check-in for your flight.
9:10 pm	Argue with check-in lady over one of the many irregularities she will allege on your ticket (you have no reservation, you have not confirmed your flight, we do not have a seat for you, we can only give you a middle seat). Bribe her if necessary to get your own way.
9:30 pm	Stand in a scrummage for another twenty minutes waiting to go through passport control.
9:50 pm	Enter the departures lounge.
10:30 pm	Discover by accident that your 10:30 p.m. flight has not been called. No information will be available. Staff will know nothing.
1:30 am	Discover by accident that your flight will take off at 2:30 am, four hours late.

Tip For Your Trip

Remember local people are always right. They have a lot of experience of these things.

70 TRAFFIC JAMS

Three hours sitting in traffic jams is the norm in unusual countries for the ten mile journey between the international airport and the city centre. This is because the government has forgotten to build the appropriate roads (see section on CORRUPTION).

The problem with flying is that it has a peculiar effect on the body's waterworks. Whilst in the air you feel continually dehydrated and therefore quite properly consume a lot of liquid.

As soon as you are on the ground and your taxi leaves the airport you realise that the change in air pressure means that the liquid no longer wants to remain in your body. It is at this precise point in time, when you feel the pressure building up in your bladder, that you realise you had made a mistake in not entering that smelly, filthy, overcrowded, wet-floored toilet in the airport arrivals area. You had thought you could wait until you arrived at the hotel, a mere ten miles from the airport. Very unwise!

So there you are, sitting in a traffic jam that is not moving and you are bursting. What do you do?

The wise thing to do is carry a urine bottle (with cork stopper) in your hand baggage. Ask your travelling companion (if you have one) to turn the other way whilst using it. Also always remember to sit in the back seat of the taxi.

You can buy urine bottles at pharmacists or at souvenir shops in hospitals.

It is best to get some practice using these urine bottles before visiting an unusual country. Back home, invite your partner to take you for a drive along a busy motorway leaving a major city on a Friday evening. Drink two litres of water before you leave and wait thirty minutes. Start the journey at 4:30 p.m. and make sure you are in a traffic jam by 5:30 p.m. Then, whilst in the back seat of the car pull down your jeans and practice using the urine bottle. Don't worry about people staring at you.

It is wise to take with you a wet sponge bag with disinfectant to mop up afterwards in case you lack precision of aim during your first practice. Alternatively use your partner's car.

Tip For Your Trip

Purchase a urine bottle with stopper before you depart and carry it with you at all times.

71 RAILWAY TRACKS

Any child knows that the shortest distance between two villages is the railway track. That is why you see so many children (and adults for that matter) walking along railway tracks in unusual countries. Furthermore, it is impossible to get lost when you walk along a railway track.

I have tried it myself on the odd occasion and find it exhilarating, especially when I do not know the railway timetables off by heart.

Fortunately in most unusual countries trains do not go very fast (it would be quicker to walk in most cases) and therefore you have plenty of time to step off the track to avoid the oncoming train. Most locals do this at the last minute as they know the train will not hit them.

Trains are cheap in these countries but not cheap enough for the poor people who have to walk along the tracks. When these poor people get tired of walking and don't have a coin for a ticket they will literally jump onto a moving train and cling to its doors (which are often left open for this very purpose). Some people climb onto the roofs to get a better view.

Overall railway travel in unusual countries can be a fascinating experience, especially if you are not too concerned about arriving on time.

It can also be incredibly cheap. None of this nonsense we have in the UK where you can pay hundreds of pounds to be a sardine in a moving can.

Tip For Your Trip

Should the opportunity arise, go by train (or air-conditioned coach as previously mentioned). Avoid single-decker buses, taxis and three-wheelers - all of which are dangerous.

Always take with you the railway timetable for the country you are in.

72 SEAT BELTS

Drivers in unusual countries are exceptionally skilled.

They are so skilled that it is totally unnecessary to wear seat-belts. In fact, most of these drivers will be grossly offended if you attempt to fasten a seat-belt. It will really hurt their professional pride.

"What do you think I am?" the driver will yell as he drives the wrong way up a street and then shoots across a red light, "a maniac?"

Even if the driver is a little more polite he will only smile at you benignly as you struggle to put on the seat-belt. If you are sitting in the back you will find the straps hidden away into the deepest recesses of the seat. As you attempt to recover the strap by digging your fingers into the cleavage between the upright and horizontal upholstery you will unearth all manner of unusual and indescribable items. It will take you years to clean your fingernails afterwards.

If you are lucky enough to find a strap you will then be unable to pull it out sufficiently to reach the buckle.

By the time you have worked out how to find and fasten the seat-belts you should be back at your hotel anyway. Unless you are stuck in a traffic jam, in which case you wouldn't have needed them in the first place.

Tip For Your Trip

I always take a long luggage strap with me when being driven by a local driver. It is easy to use. You simply loop it through the inside handle in the back door of the car, then around yourself and then back to the handle. Releasing it can be quite difficult in the event of an accident but at least you are belted up for the safe part of the journey.

73 FAST DRIVERS

As mentioned in the previous section in unusual countries local drivers are exceptionally competent. This means they can drive exceptionally fast and complete hazardous overtaking manoeuvres.

They have got driving down to a fine art. Whereas in the West we tend to allow for what we call a margin of error in unusual countries they are unaware of the concept. There is no margin of error. Just when you thought you were going to collide with the oncoming vehicle it will complete its overtaking manoeuvre and revert to the proper side of the road.

Whilst you would never dream of sitting on the tail of another car whilst driving at 80 m.p.h., drivers in unusual countries regularly do this.

These drivers, you see, are conscious that you must be punctual. It means they put their foot down all the way and only brake at the last minute unless they can swerve around an obstacle.

Traffic signs have little meaning and you should be aware that proceeding through red lights is quite standard, especially late at night when there are lots of criminals around (who will shoot if you stop).

Drivers in these countries also love to use non-verbal communication with each other. This often takes the form of shaking fists, swearing in English, sucking air through their teeth and most popular of all, hooting their horns at others. The latter happens every thirty seconds on any journey.

Lane discipline is non-existent, mainly because there are no lanes. Ducking and weaving to gain the extra inch is the order of the day. It really is a joy to watch and, if you are lucky enough, to be driven in this manner.

Tip For Your Trip

To be honest I have been terrified on many occasions at the speed at which people drive. I have therefore learnt a few polite phrases to help:

(a)   "Could you slow down a little, I would like to admire your beautiful country." (This works even in the dark when there is nothing to see).

(b) "Could you slow down a little, I would like to take a few photographs." (Also works in the dark when there is no light. However, it's useful to have a camera handy and to go through the motions).

(c) "You really would be amused to learn how we drive in England, just slow down a little and I'll tell you."

(d) "Do you know, when you get to my age I quite enjoy being driven slowly."

74 TAXIS Part I

The law of the jungle applies to taxis in most unusual countries. If there is regulation it is in name only. Before you visit any unusual country find out what the unofficial rules are relating to taxis and also find out what the standard tariff is between the airport and your hotel downtown.

There are two types of taxis, those on meters and those not on meters. Some also have meters which do not work, or work to your disadvantage. In many airports both types of taxis are available. In some countries the metered taxi is more expensive than the unmetered taxi, in other countries it is the reverse. In some countries the metered taxi is more comfortable and more reliable than the unmetered taxi, in other countries it is the reverse.

The common sense rules for using taxis are:

(i) Know the approximate fare you should be paying to your destination (the law of the jungle states that if you show any degree of ignorance about taxi fares you will be charged at least twice as much as you should be).

(ii) Agree the fare in advance and make sure it is no more than the approximate fare you have in mind.

(iii) When you wander out of the departures area pushing your luggage cart try to give an impression that you know where you are going and what you want. In many countries touts will descend upon you, take the cart out of your hand, and push it towards their taxi. Do not allow them to do this.

(iv) Have some rough idea of the route to be taken to your hotel. (Metered taxis often take you on the longest possible route).

(v) Find out if the hotel has an airport pick-up service. Most do and are pretty reliable.

In many countries taxis are run by the mafia who own the cars, charge their drivers the earth for driving them and then expect their drivers to be on the road for twenty-fours a day to make a pittance. No wonder they try to rip you off, let alone fall asleep at the wheel.

A rough rule of thumb is that it should cost you twelve dollars or seven pounds for a journey from the airport to your hotel. In most unusual countries if you want a car and driver for a day you can hire this for between forty and eighty dollars or twenty and forty pounds.

If you do think you are being ripped off refuse to pay the fare on arrival at the hotel, go to reception and ask what the standard fare is. Have cash ready, pay it to the driver and refuse to pay any more. Ten per cent of taxi drivers are exceptionally honest, very helpful and deserve a 10% tip.

Tip For Your Trip

On reflection, it's best not to use taxis in unusual countries. If you are on a tour it's easy. You'll be put on a bus and have to wait for ages until the last straggler gets on. If you insist on a car, get a friend to collect you at the airport or use the hotel pick-up service.

75 TAXIS Part 2

Most business visitors to unusual countries will not be able to afford the stretched limousines that their bosses have on their official visits. In fact, most visitors to unusual countries are not even on business trips. Instead they go as tourists.

Even so, it can be relatively boring to view the world cocooned in an air-conditioned tour bus. Thrilling opportunities will arise when you go outside your comfort zone and use local transport. For example, there will be occasions when you get lost wandering around that vast street market and return to the coach stop to find the tour bus has departed without you.

This is when you have to take your life into your own hands and use a local taxi. For a start, you can use all the negotiating skills you carefully acquired by reading the previous section.

Frequently you will find that the taxi driver is unshaven, does not speak English and will have no idea where your destination is. It is always wise, therefore, to carry with you a card printed in the local language giving the address of your hotel and a map of how to get there. Make sure the jokers at the hotel do not give you a card with the address of the local prison in the local language even if your hotel has the feel of a prison.

The small decrepit taxi you get into will be full of smoke and there will be local music blaring. It is the type of music you cannot stand and gives you headaches. The outside of the taxi will be bent and battered.

The clutch of the taxi will not be working properly and it will be a most uncomfortable ride, especially as the driver ignores all the rules of the road and frequently cuts in front of other vehicles.

The upholstery in the vehicle will be filthy and most likely torn too. Often, the windows will not wind down and one door handle will not work so you will have to get out the other side.

This is all great fun. You will, of course, be rehearsing your story for the moment you arrive back at the hotel and your fellow tourists will greet you with relief. "Where have you been?" You will treasure these adventures and tell them one thousand times. "Do you remember when we got left behind at the street market?" Such are the thrills of travel.

Tip For Your Trip

Whilst it is best not to use local taxis in unusual countries, if you are forced to do so ensure that you take with you a card with the address of your hotel printed in the local language along with a detailed map of how to get there.

76 BUSES AND TRUCKS

I have seen whole farmyards of scraggy cows, scruffy goats and scratching chickens on the tops of single-decker buses in unusual countries. And they were in first class. Below, caged like prisoners in a medieval gaol were twice as many passengers as there should be, whilst clinging to the side of the bus were hordes of reckless people risking their life and limb for a free ride.

These buses actually do move, but not very far and not very fast. They fart out huge volumes of black smoke and cause chaos as they limp along the potholed main roads. The windows on these buses are so filthy you will not be able to look out and study the urban squalor.

Once out in the countryside these buses will often break-down and then you will see masses of people standing silently alongside waiting for something to happen. Meanwhile, they have let their animals off and these wander aimlessly along the highway causing further traffic chaos.

Breakdowns are, of course, common in unusual countries. Many a time I have seen a huge overloaded truck laid up by the roadside, miles from anywhere, one wheel off and the driver asleep under the vehicle waiting for something to happen.

Truck drivers, when they can actually get their trucks going, are a total menace. They are totally unaware of the rules of the road, invariably drive vehicles that are grossly overloaded and in danger of toppling over (which they frequently do) and always drive without lights on the wrong side of the road (to avoid potholes).

Back in the city centres you will come across bus stations where there are hundreds of buses that never seem to move and ten thousand people trying to get on them, along with their cows, goats, chickens, bedrolls and ten tons of market produce.

In some of the more progressive unusual countries it is now possible to find modern air-conditioned coaches to take you from one big city to another without stopping at every village on the way. These charge exorbitant fares and are intended for professional people as well as people from abroad who believe that they are experiencing life like the locals by using public transport.

Tip For Your Trip

Only use modern air-conditioned coaches in unusual countries.

77 THREE-WHEELERS

If you want to experience all the thrills of the funfair and particularly the dodgems then visit an unusual country and hire a three-wheeler. These are sometimes called tuk-tuks, trishaws, tricycles or triwheels depending on the country you are in. They normally have a roof of canvas but no windows and no seat-belts. Passenger are exposed to the elements, or to be exact to the pollutants.

Three-wheeler drivers will give you a fantastically dangerous ride weaving in and out of the traffic. They will squeeze between a bus and a truck just as you thought you were about to be transformed into a moving sandwich. Have faith, you will survive, ignore local newspaper reports about occasional fatalities.

Drivers will do U-turns in the face of fast moving oncoming traffic. They will ignore all the rules of the road and only stop thirty seconds and thirty yards after you thought they should have stopped.

Three-wheeler drivers are normally very friendly and spend most of the journey looking backwards at you, chatting away and trying to persuade you to visit their best friend's brothel. You have to understand they will get a 10% commission for this.

One tuk-tuk ride I had entailed a half-hour negotiation with the driver who tried to convince me the shopping mall I wanted to visit was too expensive, old-fashioned and not very good. He was insisting I go to another mall where I could buy cheap shirts (his brother owned the shop). It was then that he said he could arrange for a girl to be sent to my hotel room. He was full of similarly useful suggestions.

Finally, when I arrived at the shopping mall I asked him how much? At last he smiled sweetly and told me it was up to me to pay him what I wanted.

So I pulled out a wad of 100 unit notes and gave him two hundred. "Three hundred will do," he told me, eyeing the wad. I gave him the extra hundred. The hotel limousine had charged me two hundred for the same journey. But I wasn't going to argue over half a dollar.

Tip For Your Trip

Unless you enjoy the thrills of the dodgems avoid riding in three-wheelers.

78 STRANGE TOILETS (Part 3)

Frequent flyers may be surprised to learn that in certain unusual countries long journeys still have to be taken by road. There aren't even any railway lines. Furthermore, that thick red line on the map between two major cities will not be what you expect. If you are expecting a motorway, an interstate highway or an autobahn then you will be bitterly disappointed. In some unusual countries you will be lucky to get a stretch of tarmac to be driven along. Nor should you expect to find friendly service areas where you can have a pee and relax with a can of ice-cold cola and a juicy cheeseburger.

This is all right for those of you who are adventurous and who are keen to see miles and miles of boring countryside, of barren brown fields and scrubland with the occasional tree to relieve the monotony.

However those of you who welcome the comforts of life will find such long journeys rather arduous. Let us take toilets for example. There aren't any. If they do exist they are very strange. On your two hundred mile journey you will occasionally come across a village. The one toilet in this village will be a hole in the ground surrounded by a flimsy wickerwork fence and a door that blows open. In the poorer villages there will be no fence and no door.

The other option is to try the unspeakable toilets at the back of the petrol (gas) stations that are dotted along the road every forty miles. These toilets are cleaned at least once year, stink to high heaven, are infested with flies and indescribably filthy.

You should only use unspeakable toilets if something more unspeakable is about to happen to you and the clothes that you are wearing.

Or, you could follow the example of my driver on my last trip down south in an unusual country. He turned to me and said "I stop now, I urinate". He stopped on the side of the road, got out and then urinated against the back wheel. This is behaviour that I have seen on many occasions but only locals are allowed to do this.

Tip For Your Trip

The secret to long journeys is preparation. The best course of action is not to eat any breakfast on the day you are travelling, nor any lunch. You should not consume any liquid either. You should fast until you have arrived at the end of the eight hour drive and are within easy reach of a toilet that has been cleaned in the last month.

If you become dehydrated on your journey then drink a can of warm cola. This is the only emergency precaution I would advise.

79 SLEEPING DRIVERS

I had hired a driver for a sightseeing trip. As there were no modern highways in this unusual country the roads were unspeakably narrow with lots of traffic and very little overtaking space. This did not stop people overtaking.

I'd had no breakfast and was starving. We drove through a coastal village and my driver pointed out what seemed like a decent restaurant and suggested we stop there for lunch. I decided to go against my own advice and risk eating.

With my customary hospitality I invited the driver to join me at the table. He was too embarrassed to decline my offer yet equally embarrassed to accept as his English was poor. However, he knew he would benefit from two lunches; the one I paid for and the free one provided by the restaurant owner for introducing a customer to his restaurant.

Putting it more succinctly, my driver ate a lot: two plates of rice and two huge portions of chicken. I ate less, but even so the lunch induced a state of sleepiness on my part as we drove back towards the capital. I began to doze off in the passenger seat.

I suddenly awoke from my stupor to find we were driving on the wrong side of the road with a big truck heading towards us. I relaxed thinking my driver was doing just another one of his dangerous overtaking manoeuvres from which on every previous occasion we had emerged unscathed.

However, on this occasion I noticed something unusual. My driver had his eyes shut. Yes, this is true. He was driving whilst asleep. He was in automatic mode. Now, when I was a child I used to sleepwalk and wake up to find myself in a wardrobe (closet) peeing into my mother's shoes. My parents were always very understanding. But sleep-driving is far removed from sleepwalking in terms of danger.

With the driver still asleep a split second passed. Instinctively, I coughed and asked him "How long before we get back?" He awoke instantly and automatically guided the car back to the right lane, thus narrowly missing the truck by inches.

I opened the window to let in some fresh air hoping this would keep him awake but he told me to keep it closed as it was dangerous in the next town and people had a habit of putting hands through windows when the car stopped at lights.

So, for the final hour of this journey, I kept an eye on my driver who consistently failed to keep an eye on the road as he reverted often to sleep. I exhausted my repertoire of wake-up call interrupts. Mercifully, we eventually arrived safely.

Tip For Your Trip

After lunch always keep an eye on the driver of your coach, car or taxi. Try to sit in the front seat and if you see him going to sleep have a question ready to shout at him!

80 WAITING

One of the best things about visiting unusual countries is that you have to spend a lot of time waiting around, sometimes hours on end, if not days on end. During these periods you will have ample opportunity to reflect on the bad old days back home when you were constantly rushing around, very stressed and never had time enough for anything.

In unusual countries you can de-stress yourself, for example, by taking full advantage of flight delays between six and twenty-four hours. It is an excellent opportunity to swat for exams, catch up on reading and write postcards. Whether you go to the bank, go shopping, visit a restaurant or attempt to buy a ticket at a railway station, in an unusual country be prepared to wait. At banks the average waiting time is three hours. The wait will not necessarily be comfortable as there will be heaving crowds and dim lights. It will also be hot and humid. The same applies to post offices and public hospitals.

It is no good complaining about the wait, this will only make you (nobody else) feel worse. In unusual countries you have to learn to feel good about waiting. Everything takes a long time in unusual countries.

Even trying to make a purchase at a bookshop can require quite a wait. Having chosen the book from the limited selection you will have to wait ten minutes for an assistant to write you a ticket. He will keep the book whilst you trek to another counter with your ticket and wait another ten minutes to pay for your book. You will then return to the original counter and wait for a third time to collect your purchase.

The culture of most unusual countries is based on the principle of waiting. If you are a local and applying for a job then you can wait for days outside an office for an interview.

The underlying principle of waiting is that if you wait long enough something will happen. Thus, if you wait long enough on the roadside a bus will come along. It might take four hours or four days, but eventually the bus will come.

The key is to feel positive about waiting. You will have plenty of time to think about what life is all about and may eventually write a book about it.

Tip For Your Trip

Always carry with you a large notebook in which you can jot down those brilliant innovative thoughts you have whilst waiting around. Also carry with you the Complete Works of Shakespeare for light reading when you have even more waiting to do.

81 MAPS AND MAIL

Maps do exist in unusual countries but often they are not too helpful. The main reason is that many roads do not have names. Furthermore, many houses do not have numbers. Such labelling of roads and houses is an alien concept in many cultures.

Most rich people in unusual countries have designated post boxes from which they are supposed to collect their mail. But as mail delivery is so sporadic they don't often bother. This is why you rarely get a reply to the letters you send. As letters don't arrive. It's also a good reason for not paying your taxes.

The reason the mail doesn't arrive is for one of the following reasons:

(a)   Letters are used by post office staff to fuel incinerators (given the fuel shortages that exist in many of these countries).

(b)   Post office workers just can't be bothered to do anything about the accumulating bags of mail.

(c)   When post office workers are bothered they open the mail to see if there is anything worth stealing from it.

(d)   Then the postal workers discard the worthless letters and envelopes (for burning).

(e)   Postal workers collect picture stamps from around the world and tear these off (never ever send a letter to an unusual country with a picture stamp on it).

(f)   Post office workers cannot read.

(g)   All mail is censored by government spies who then forget to mail it on.

(h)   If a letter does not have a P O Box number on it post office workers do not know where the address is let alone the mailbox.

To find people's homes first time can be exceptionally trying. You tend to get verbal directions like "Take the airport road and then the second left after the statue of the president. Go to the top of the hill and then the second on the right past the next statue of the president. Halfway down the hill you will see a large white villa with black wrought iron gates. That's where the president's mistress lives. Drive on until you come across a tall white wall with barbed wire at the end of which is a rusting iron gate with an Alsatian dog barking at you. This is where we live."

Except there is no second left before the statue of the president let alone any second statue or Alsatian dog barking. (They thought of course was that you would be coming from the opposite direction).

Tip For Your Trip

I always find a compass quite handy for navigating around countries where maps are useless. I suggest you take one with you.

82 CHECKPOINTS

Part of the fun of visiting unusual countries is endangering your life at army checkpoints. These can spring up anywhere and it is advisable to slow down when approaching one and, if necessary, stop.

You will struggle to work out the reason for most checkpoints as the soldiers there normally just wave you through without even a glance at your car. The whole process adds no value to the safety and security of the country and is probably intended to keep people gainfully employed. Sometimes there is a simple barrier across the road, other times a stretched rope which they will drop to let you through. More often than not it is just an army truck by the side of the road with a couple of unshaven rifle-carrying soldiers lounging around with fags hanging out of their mouths.

There are occasions when one of these soldiers will wave you down and then glance inside your car before beckoning you on. If it is dark he will wave a torch momentarily inside the car. It is advisable to be polite and co-operative every time this happens. I have even had the experience of having these soldiers ask for my papers and pretend to study them.

In other words, most checkpoints are innocuous and this is the danger. For every ninety-nine innocuous checkpoints there is a dangerous one. At the dangerous one they will demand money (better known as a present). If you refuse you will be shot and your possessions and car will be stolen. Your body will simply disappear. Soldiers are good at this type of thing.

Most people prefer to co-operate and will have twenty dollars ready (the normal price) to preserve their life.

The cleverer soldiers will seriously try to find something wrong with your papers, or your car and then fine you. You can be guaranteed if they are looking for something wrong they will find it.

In my humble, albeit experienced, opinion these are not occasions for principles but matters of life and death. Whatever the principles involved, personally I would not forsake my life for twenty dollars (especially if I can write about it later).

Tip For Your Trip

Always ensure you have at least one hundred twenty dollar bills with you.

83 HEADLIGHTS

In the UK we have a quaint habit of giving way to other drivers.

For non-UK readers I should explain that when driving along a main road in Scotland, Wales and England (excepting London) a driver will slow down when he or she sees another car waiting to exit from a side road. The kind UK driver on the main road will flash his headlights. The other driver on the side road will see this and then cautiously enter the main road without fear of being hit by the approaching car.

It is for this reason alone that the British people are renowned around the world for their sense of fair play, good manners and common decency.

Experienced British drivers will thus interpret a flashing headlight as an invitation to proceed in front of the oncoming vehicle.

It is very important that you know that the reverse applies in unusual countries.

I am writing this in an unusual country and have just witnessed three other drivers flashing lights at my rather Anglicised local driver who, at my request, drives slowly and sedately. This flash of headlights simply means 'Get out of my bloody way otherwise I will crush you'. This is their way of extending a simple courtesy to prevent you from dying (which is so commonplace in these countries).

As the driver flashes his lights (it is rare to find female drivers in these countries) he will speed up and come straight at you. He will have total faith that you will get out of his way. You do. This sort of trust in other drivers moving out of your way is implicit in unusual countries.

So there you are. It is that simple. Get out of the way of flashing headlights. You risk entering a permanent state of forgetfulness if unfortunately you forget you are in an unusual country and still think you are in the UK.

Tip For Your Trip

When driving in unusual countries take with you a sticker to place inside your windscreen. Remember to get out of the way of drivers flashing their headlights.

Remember to take with you your UK driving license. (The more endorsements it has, the more the local police will be impressed).

Yes, we do have women drivers in the UK and sometimes they are as polite, if not more so, than male drivers. Mainly because they drive so slowly and safely.

84 PLANE CRASHES

Planes do not crash in unusual countries as often as you think. But they do crash, and more often than they do back home. These are normally on internal flights within the country where the high standards of international flights do not apply.

The main reason for these crashes is that the airlines cannot afford to maintain their aircraft properly nor do they have sufficiently trained engineers. This is what the pilots say.

The engineers will tell you it's not like that at all. They will tell you stories of the co-pilot going for a nap in first class and then the captain going to get himself a coffee in the galley and absent-mindedly locking himself and the co-pilot out of the cockpit, thus leaving the plane pilotless. Or they will tell you of a pilot allowing his young son to fly the aircraft, or of a captain and his second in command spending most of the flight chatting up the beautiful stewardesses in first class.

Whatever the reason, flying internally in unusual countries can be a thrilling experience. More often than not planes do not crash. This is because they do not take off in the first place. Delays of up to twenty-four hours are quite common. Cancellations are even more frequent.

Airlines in unusual countries often run out of aeroplanes or the parts that go into them. On occasions they also run out of fuel.

A more frequent occurrence is when the airline runs out of food. This does not stop them from flying. When this happens you are lucky to get a glass of water mid-flight, even if you are in first-class.

When flying internally in unusual countries it is advisable not to use the plane's strange toilets (this could cause a crash) or try to adjust your seat (which could cause the plane to arrive at the wrong destination). Do not expect to find a seat-belt that works or any announcements which make sense.

Having flown on many internal flights in unusual countries I always reassure people that I have not been in a crash yet.

The key is to be positive. I have been told that you are more likely to be run over by a red double-decker bus than killed in a plane crash. But then .... they don't have red double-decker buses in unusual countries!

Tip For Your Trip

When taking internal flights in unusual countries always read the latest book on positive thinking.

CHAPTER 6

THE PEOPLE YOU MEET IN UNUSUAL COUNTRIES AND THEIR CUSTOMS

There is no point in travelling to unusual countries if all you want to do is see breathtaking scenery, spectacular mountains, wondrous waterfalls, historic temples, tribal dancing or to lie on paradise beaches. Such activities are so common in this modern age that they hardly merit a mention. All you end up with is a list:

Grand Canyon:	Had scary helicopter ride, done that.
Rocky Mountains:	Very cloudy but saw one or two peaks, done that.
Niagara Falls:	Tried to see it but it was foggy, even so done that.
Wall Street:	Walked down, it took two minutes, done that.
Tribal dancing:	Photographed a few tits, done that.
Miami beach:	Too dangerous to swim, but posed for photos, done that.
Windsor Castle:	Too close to home. Do that next year.
Tower of London:	Too busy when I'am in London. Do that next year etc. etc.

What is really fascinating about unusual countries is the people you meet and their rather unusual customs. They are totally unlike those boring people you meet back home. Instead they exhibit behaviour which is very different to ours.

In this chapter we take a few glimpses at one or two of these unusual people and their customs.

85 BRIBERY

Bribery is quite acceptable in unusual countries, especially to those people accepting it. In fact, bribery is one of those quaint customs people in unusual countries have. We also have it in the UK for acquiring peerages.

I would go so far as to say that nothing gets done in unusual countries without a little bit of bribery. If you want to stick to your principles fine, but you will get nowhere!

Bribery comes in quite useful for the following activities:

(a) Saving the time of customs officials. In the absence of bribery, customs officials can spend at least thirty minutes going through every item in your tightly-packed luggage looking for something to be confiscated (in lieu of a bribe).

(b) Passing through immigration control. In the absence of bribery, the immigration officer will slowly study every single page of your passport before passing it to one of his colleagues for a similar study. It's best to fasten, with a paper clip, a ten dollar note to the relevant page. This speeds things up considerably if you are rushing to catch a plane.

(c) Jumping a three hour queue (anywhere).

(d) Getting the hotel room you thought you had booked but which the hotel staff are convinced you hadn't, despite your piece of paper confirming your reservation.

(e) Persuading security guards to allow unofficial visitors into your hotel bedroom.

(f) Getting a seat on an aeroplane at check-in even when you have a confirmed reservation.

(g) Getting any type of upgrade.

(h) Getting jobs done which normally should be done for free.

(i) Getting a visa (if you suddenly decide to visit a neighbouring unusual country).

(j) Getting a form for a visa application.

(k) Getting into the embassy to ask for a visa application form.

(l) In lieu of hefty fines for any type of traffic offence.

(m) Avoiding being thrown in gaol.

In some countries bribery is better known as dash whereas in other countries it is difficult to differentiate bribery from tipping.

It is important to realise that in unusual countries bribery rarely takes place in local currency (of which you will have none on arrival). To facilitate bribery throughout the world there is a universal law that requires it to be done in US dollars. Dollars are highly prized and will ensure that you receive much better value for money in your chosen pursuit than if you try to use another currency.

Tip For Your Trip

Take a least two hundred single dollar notes on your trip for the purpose of bribery.

86 CORRUPTION

Whilst bribery is quite acceptable in unusual countries corruption does not exist. You can speak to any senior politician, army general or owner of a major company and they will categorically deny that corruption exists in their country, in fact you will probably be thrown in gaol for having the audacity to suggest it.

In these countries it would be totally wrong, for example, to approach a senior person and make an offer such as "There is a 10% cut in this for you if you ensure the decision goes in my favour."

As we all know, this would be an insult to the person you approach. He undoubtedly prides himself on his immense integrity and would be shocked to think that you were trying to corrupt him. The official records, if available, will show that this person draws very little salary and that is more than proof that he is not corrupt. It will, of course, be understood that these senior people have to lavish a lot on expenses in order to keep up appearances with the high and mighty of this world. This might require multimillion dollar homes around the world and private jets to hop around the globe. It is important to remember that these are important people who are very busy and these perks go naturally with the job.

The following types of gestures would, of course, be perfectly acceptable in unusual countries and should in no way be considered as corruption:

(a) "Judge, as a gesture of appreciation for all the hard work that I know you are going to put into my legal dispute with that rogue I would like to offer you and your wife or mistress two complimentary first class return plane tickets to my home country together with a ten night stay at a five star hotel, all expenses paid."

(b) "Minister, I understand that you own a small private consultancy firm run by your son. I thought you ought to know that should we win this major contract then we will be awarding your consultancy firm a million dollar assignment to provide us with advice on the implementation of the contract."

(c) "General, I understand that you will be retiring soon and this will be one of the last procurement decisions you make. You know that our equipment is the best in the world and that it will be a mere formality to award us the contract. After retirement we would like to employ you as an adviser to our company. This will involve a fair amount of first class foreign travel with, of course, unlimited expenses. You will receive a small salary and additional bonuses will be paid in due course relating to the success of our business in this part of the world."

Tip For Your Trip

Should you be travelling to an unusual country on business it is wise to carry with you at least four open first class return plane tickets to any city to which the rich are attracted.

87 PUNCTUALITY

Punctuality is a peculiarly Western concept and has relatively little meaning to people in unusual countries.

This is because people gear their lives to their own sense of time rather than anyone else's. As most locals have no sense of time it doesn't really matter anyway.

If you are not used to this attitude you will initially find it frustrating. For example, if someone says "Please come around to dinner this evening" and you ask what time, they will say eight o'clock - the first thing that comes into their head. You will then worry what they actually mean by eight o'clock - proving it was a stupid question that you asked in the first place! The answer is that it doesn't really matter what time you arrive - as long it is not eight o'clock. It is even in order not to turn up at all, or even turn up after the dinner is finished.

What normally happens is that the hostess and her servants wait for a sufficient number of people to appear and then they start cooking. This normally takes two hours. When you are just about to leave they start serving the food.

Normally allow at least one hour for leaving. It is when you start leaving that people start to remember all the things they wanted to tell you and as you go around kissing each person's cheeks three times they will each retain you for five minutes to give advice and tell you things they had forgotten to mention in the previous six hours.

You will find that most things are done at the last minute, like arriving at the airport. In unusual countries there is never enough time to do whatever is necessary.

Amongst the more educated people there is a thing called British time. Occasionally, if you invite someone to visit you at the hotel and specify a time they will ask whether this is local time or do you mean British time? With British time you are allowed to be up to half an hour late only. However, you should only specify British time on very special occasions. For routine everyday things just ignore the timings people give you and do your own thing. It's much more relaxed and much more fun than the extremely stressful rush we have, why is there a need to do things on time anyway?

Tip For Your Trip

Wear two watches. On your left hand should be one set to local time and on the right hand one set to British time (albeit this should never be the GMT or BST we have back in the UK).

88 BEGGARS

When visiting many unusual countries you will be accosted by beggars outside the buildings you are visiting. Some times these beggars have hideous deformities or are in a pitiful state. You will see sights that appal you. Often the beggars will be teenage mums cradling sleeping kids in their arms. In some countries the beggars are as young as five years old. They are called street kids as they live on the streets by themselves with no parents or social carers to look after them. They ply the streets late at night when their earnings can be maximised.

Should you toss a beggar a coin then out of nowhere fifty others will appear demanding a coin too. Each will be in rags, have pleading eyes and will be thrusting their hands at you. When in a traffic jam a beggar may come hammering on your window, screaming "master, master" and hoping to get you to open your window and give him a coin. You learn, regrettably, to avoid eye contact. Once you establish eye contact you feel guilty if you don't give. Eye contact humanises.

In most unusual countries begging is much better organised than any social services the local authorities can provide. People boss the beggars around, take their own personal cut and have a system for designating a patch to each beggar. With their extensive on-the-job training beggars have learnt that there is only one effective tactic and this is to make you feel as bad as they appear to be. They want to make you suffer in the way that you think they are suffering. Therefore, the only way to make yourself feel better is to make them feel better. In other words they work at your conscience.

And it works. I'd hate to be a beggar. During my travels I have seen thousands and they always sadden me. I always come to the conclusion that I'd rather be me than them. Despite my huge credit card debts the fact is I am better off than them. So I toss a few coins to as many as I can which in reality means an incredibly small minority. At least it makes me feel better.

It literally is impossible to give money to every beggar you come across and you are therefore forced to limit yourself. I make sure that in the course of each day I collect as much small change as possible. Then I dispose of this small change in the most equitable way possible, albeit I tend to favour those beggars who are making a conscious effort to do something useful (like playing music, dancing, juggling or offering a few kind words).

Even with the bags of small change I toss out I am forced to fob off the majority of beggars. I cannot please them all no matter how much it would please me. If I gave away a million dollars in small change I don't think it would make the slightest difference to the beggars and their community. That's the paradox.

Tips For Your Trip

Collect coins in unusual countries and deposit them in a large purse which you should carry at all times. Try to give away some money every day. Some people advise it is better to give food (cartons of milk, or packs of cookies) than money.

89 HAWKERS

One rung up the social ladder from beggars are hawkers. If you are accosted every minute of the day by a beggar then you will be accosted every thirty seconds by a hawker.

This happens when you venture into city centres, onto beaches or visit any tourist site. Hawkers come up to you offering you cheap trinkets, fake watches, grotty souvenirs, postcards, Viagra and many other things. It also happens at road junctions where there are huge traffic jams and also at border crossings.

I was at one such border post in a remote[1] part of the world and my driver had gone off to get my papers processed and my passport stamped. As usual this took more than half an hour. Meanwhile, he had left me in the car which was parked on a section of wasteland by the border post (all border posts in unusual countries are surrounded by wasteland).

Whilst waiting I got out of the car to stretch my legs. As soon as I did so half a dozen young boys descended upon me trying to sell me pirated CDs, chewing gum, disposable cigarette lighters, pastries and soft drinks. My instinct as always was to wave them away.

Yet, one young man was more persistent than usual. He was carrying a heavy tray of pirated CDs and, despite my constant refusal, kept offering me one CD after another. First Whitney Houston, then Kenny Rogers, Bob Marley, Santana, and on it went. I didn't need any CDs.

Suddenly I realised how negative I was being. I had got myself into the usual rejection mode. I started asking this young man some questions. He had travelled on foot two hundred miles from another country, with his father, to find work at this border crossing. He was fourteen and he spoke four languages (English, French and two local languages). He might sell three or four CDs a day if he was lucky. He was charging four dollars (negotiable down to two dollars) per CD.

This was his living and here I was denying him it, refusing him two dollars when it was nothing to me. He was trying and I was resisting despite the fact that life was a thousand times tougher for him than me.

[1] Nearest airport 500 miles away

Suddenly my whole mindset changed. Why was I being so difficult? So I bought four of the CDs. To this day I have never played them. The lesson I learnt is that when someone is desperate for a sale it is often wise to buy even if you don't need the item being purchased. The amount of money involved is next to nothing.

Tip For Your Trip

Do something for poor people. Buy items from hawkers even if you do not need them.

90 GIVING

Continuing in the philosophical vein of the last two sections it is important when travelling within an unusual country to adopt a giving attitude.

Remember that most of the people you meet will not know about your overdraft or your horrendous credit card debts and will view you as rich. They would be staggered to learn that what you earn in one week they earn in one year if they are lucky.

They will see from your clothes and the way that you walk and talk that you are different from them. You will have travelled from an exotic country about which they know little, although they aspire to visiting it one day.

Therefore you must go all out to give. Do not restrain your giving instincts when travelling in these countries. Do not be frightened to hand a coin to a beggar, or to take a case full of small gifts (for example pens) to hand out as appropriate.

Do not hesitate to offer to buy the drinks or lunch if a local person invites you. Your host might well refuse and a fight might ensue (always give in) but it is important to make the gesture.

However, the biggest gift you can make is to take a genuine interest in the people you are with. Do not assume that where you come from is the fount of all wisdom in this world. You will be totally wrong. The people you meet in unusual countries have levels of wisdom which you will have never encountered previously in your life. Listen carefully and learn from them. You might not think their way is the best (and this book might have given you that impression) but conversely do not assume that your way is the best - at least in their eyes. It could just be that the West is more decadent.

Learn about their approach to family, learn about their approach to dealing with adversity and deprivation, learn about their approach to integrity.

The major benefit of travelling is to learn from other people. It is worth all the inconveniences and petty frustrations listed in this book. It is worth having a rat in your room when you can learn about the rats back in your own country, and there are many!

Tip For Your Trip

Never stop giving to people. Every day give something away especially when visiting an unusual country. Give a coin, a carton of milk, a pen, a business card (much prized by local people), a photograph, a book or a toy. Collect and keep the give-aways you often get at home (the things they hand out at major railway stations or in shopping malls) and take these with you to give away. Other examples are the shampoos, toiletries and stationery found in your hotel room. Give them away!

91 TIPPING

Tipping is an excellent idea in unusual countries. It is wise to tip everyone who does anything for you, except the manager or owner of the establishment, and even then it may be appropriate on occasion.

Failing to tip is a dreadful idea in unusual countries. Your worst nightmares will come true when you fail to tip. For a start, the word will get around the locality that you are mean and that you deserve no help at all. The lights in your bedroom will go off mysteriously and will never ever come on again without of course, a massive tip. You will not be served breakfast, full stop. You will not be able to make a telephone call. Your wake-up calls will not come. Taxi drivers will chase you for the next three hours.

As stated in the previous sections when you set foot in an unusual country people will assume that you are rich. Local people have this idea that rich people do nothing for themselves. Everything is done for them. You will not be allowed to carry a bag, open a door, shop for a newspaper, walk from one end of the street to the other without some person offering to do it for you. They will even switch on the television for you and expect a tip (this is worth it because most televisions in unusual countries are difficult to turn on).

People will guard your car and expect a tip. Without a tip you will have no car. People will grab your shopping bag and carry it for you and then expect a tip. Without a tip you will have no shopping bag. People will come up to you and show you the way to wherever you are going, even if you have been there one hundred times before. And then they will expect a tip. Without a tip you will never get there. People will find you a taxi and expect a tip. And then the taxi driver will expect a tip (over and above the inflated fare he has charged you). Then the doorman will expect a tip. And on it goes.

Mercifully, you do not have to tip much. As mentioned previously in this learned guide a few coins is more than adequate. Bear in mind that most of the people you encounter are earning no more than two dollars a day so whatever you tip them is worth fifty times more to them than to you.

A generous tip can keep an employee and his extended family in essential supplies for one whole week. So it is worth doing.

Tip For Your Trip

When in doubt, tip.

92 BARGAINING

Part of the fun of travelling to unusual countries is to bargain for items you don't really need - for example rugs, dolls, trinkets, wooden sculptures and watches that don't work.

We are all exceptionally skilled at this fine art and will always arrive home full of heroic stories of how we bargained this trader down from fifty dollars to thirty dollars or obtained 50% off the sale price.

We also know that it is the biggest con in the world. These traders have degrees in psychology and know that it is essential to make you feel good and give you an excellent story to take home along with the item purchased. Their skill is to judge the degree to which they should screw you whilst giving the pretence that you are screwing them.

Rest assured that whatever you pay you are paying too much. Most of the products they are selling are worthless (trying selling them on eBay when back home).

I have items in my loft which I've purchased abroad that I can't even give away.

Even so, if you persist in purchasing rubbish abroad (just for the story) here is a general rule of thumb:

(a)   If the ticket price is less than $20 don't bargain. It's not worth the effort.

(b)   If the ticket price is between $20 and $100 aim to get 30% off.

(c)   If the ticket price is higher than $100 aim to get 50% off.

The only real way to bargain is not to genuinely want the item in the first place and to show total disinterest in it. (Which begs the question of why try to buy it?) The higher the interest you show in the item the more you will pay. In bargaining, show total indifference towards what you might be buying and drive the trader down to the lowest possible price. Then say it's too high, goodbye and start to walk away. The trader will then come chasing after you and offer you an even lower price. You might then just be tempted even though you don't want the item.

It is always wise to shop around and compare prices. This isn't difficult as all traders are selling the same things.

Tip For Your Trip

During the long flight to the unusual country it is worth studying a DVD on negotiating skills.

93 CHANGE

Nobody ever has any change in unusual countries. Try to buy anything from street-sellers or stallholders in the market and they will shake their head when you ask for change from a 1000 unit note.

They will empty their pockets and go through an elaborate ritual pretending to look for coins or small denomination notes they can give you. They will slam open the till and rummage around knowing full well there are no coins there. They will search everywhere, in boxes, in corners. They will ask their friends, they will ask neighbouring traders. But no change will be found. Taxi drivers are the same.

All this can take up to ten minutes. It might take you a long time to get the message but they will be delighted when you raise your hand and say forget it!

Some mean-minded visitors do insist on only paying the price they have agreed. What I sometimes do is go to the hotel cashier as soon as I arrive and ask to change three 1000 unit notes into small denominations and change. Hotel cashiers are the only people in the world who will give you this change. You can try at a bank but in unusual countries you can wait up to three hours to be served. To be honest it's not worth waiting this long for a few coins and some grubby notes worth ten cents.

Once you are armed with a big wad of low denomination notes or a hefty bag of coins you are in a great position to pay the exact price agreed. However, carrying such large volumes of money around does make you vulnerable to mugging. So you can't really win anyway.

Tip For Your Trip

Never forget to carry a large purse with you and always remember to obtain some change as soon as you arrive at the hotel.

94 MONEY CHANGERS

The best customer service in any unusual country is provided by money-changers. This is because they want your money. As such, there are a lot of them around and they are all chasing your business. When I came out of customs at the airport recently there were at least six money-changers with incredibly friendly people shouting "Good afternoon sir, good flight? Change money? I offer you the best rate. No commission." And they all did offer the best rate. In fact, they all offered exactly the same rate down to the last cent.

You can guarantee that the best rate is far better than that offered by your hotel. In turn, the hotel rate will be better than those exploitative profiteering sods at your own bank which will give you the worst rate of all. I am absolutely appalled by the low rates my own bank offers. Before departing on this particular trip I was foolish enough to order one hundred pounds of local currency. I received eight hundred and twenty units. On arrival I could have exchanged the same hundred pounds for eight hundred and ninety units.

That's why I prefer to use backstreet money-changers in unusual countries. They all offer you the best price and it is. And none of them charge you commission. They count the money out in front of you and never once have they counted it incorrectly even though they count it very fast.

Furthermore, they all smile and most of them are open twenty-four hours a day, seven days a week which is more than can be said for my miserable bank back home.

Finally, in dealing with local money-changers there is none of this nonsense about having to queue for ages as you do with those horrible banks back home.

Tip For Your Trip

Exchange your home currency in the unusual country, but never with a UK bank. Don't waste your time and money with traveller's cheques either.

95 YOUR BEST FRIEND

Every other person you meet in an unusual country is your best friend. I have made so many best friends I have forgotten who most of them are. Occasionally after my return I have sent them a letter but they never reply. Few of them have email.

When you step outside your hotel to stretch your legs your best friend will be there fobbing off the beggars and hawkers in an effort to protect you. You might not have met him before but he is still your best friend. He will tell you his name and then accompany you so that he can show you the sights, help you shop and possibly sell you a few trinkets he has up his sleeve or hidden in his hanky.

He will speak excellent English and claim to have many friends in your home country. He will know all the local traders and how to get you the best deal whatever it is. I have been told that your best friend will even procure women for you but I have never tested this. I suspect that it is true.

He will be so insistent on being your best friend that he will refuse to be shaken off, unless of course, you give him some money.

The other types of best friends you encounter on your travels will be people who sit next to you on aeroplanes. In the space of an hour or two you can get to know them intimately and even get to like them. But two weeks later they will cease to exist and will have forgotten who you are if you try to contact them.

Business acquaintances can also be your best friends whilst you are visiting unusual countries to work. They will go out of their way to help you (the sort of thing we never do back in our country) and confide in you all manner of things. They will take a great interest in you, your family and what is happening back in your own home country. Furthermore, they will be incredibly hospitable. But as soon as you return home they will forget about you, fail to respond to emails and generally be unavailable when you call.

It is generally advisable to act as a best friend to everyone when visiting an unusual country. You can make as many promises as you like, nobody really expects you to keep them. You can say whatever you like, nobody ever really listens. You can lie as much as you like because they will never check you out, even when they don't believe you. You can say you know the president and they will accept it.

Generally these people are very wise. They offer the hand of friendship because they know that when you return home that friendship will cease to exist until such time as the next favour is required.

Tip For Your Trip

Take with you at least 100 personalised name cards with you to hand to your best friends. Any name will do.

96 EXPATRIATES

If you spend long enough socialising with strangers in unusual countries you will eventually encounter an eccentric subspecies from the UK called an expatriate. They are better known by the locals as "big snapper fish in small lake we piss in" or "he with nose of chocolate caramel."

Expatriates are very easy to recognise by the following behaviour:

(a) They only socialise with other expatriates of the same nationality.

(b) They never socialise with locals.

(c) They pretend to be pally with their servants whilst treating them abysmally.

(d) On weekdays they never start drinking before sundown.

(e) After sundown they never stop drinking (normally gin and tonic).

(f) They have wives who gossip and backbite over coffee every single morning of the week.

(g) They have children in expensive private schools back home.

(h) They know absolutely everything about the country they are in.

(i) They complain about how dreadful everything is in 'this' country.

(j) They will tell you how they can get nothing in 'this' country and have to import all their luxuries from home.

(k) They spend weekends at the country club where they play a little tennis, laze around the swimming pool, read last week's European papers and start drinking at midday.

(m) They are all incredibly superficial,non intellectual, loudmouthed, self-righteous, patronising, condescending, pompous, paternalistic, autocratic and basically stupid. (If you are an expatriate reading this then you are an exception).

Unless you are a tourist making a short visit to the country it is unlikely that you will be able to avoid expatriates in these unusual places.

If you do attempt to mix with the locals the resident expatriates will think you very queer and will quickly ostracise you, leaving you to your own devices during your visit. This might be preferable.

There is no known antidote to expatriate alienation.

Tip For Your Trip

Avoid expatriates and avoid becoming one.

97 LOCAL BOSSES

When visiting an unusual country it is impossible to avoid local bosses, whether you are a tourist, a student or on some work project. These local bosses are very important people. You can recognise them immediately because they will always dress better than you. They will have immaculate pinstriped suits and heavily starched pure white shirts with really elegant tasteful silk ties. They will also be dripping in gold with gold teeth, gold cufflinks, gold watches, gold bracelets and gold tie-pins. Even their wives and mistresses will be dripping in gold.

They will also think that they are worth their weight in gold. They will command the biggest offices and the prettiest secretaries. Modern art will adorn the walls of their offices which will have the most comfortable leather armchairs ever.

As a visitor you will be served tea in the most delicate china and they will humour you with pleasant smiles and chit-chat for a whole morning before rushing you off to lunch in their plush air-conditioned Mercedes. As you pass the slums outside and glide effortlessly over the potholes you will realise that this is what these bosses do for a living. They play at being important. They learnt this from their colonial masters a few decades back.

Back in the office they will be nice to you and horrible to everyone else, shouting commands at their employees and blaming them for anything you dare spot is wrong. These bosses will agree with everything you say and assure you that they are doing everything head office requires of them. You will, of course, never be able to verify this nor will they be able to prove it. The last thing they want is for you to get at the truth.

These bosses will earn high salaries and much more besides. They will take themselves off to every available conference around the world and, therefore, be totally familiar with all the latest techniques and theories - which they never put into practice.

When occasionally these bosses have to report poor financial results they will have a stream of ready-made excuses to hand to convince you that it is not their fault. The normal excuses made in unusual countries are: currency problems and adverse exchange rates, government restrictions, taxes, traffic jams, lack of head office support, declining markets, new competition, low rates of pay, political uncertainty, economic uncertainty, crime, corruption, bureaucracy, lack of infrastructure, trade unions, lack of education, skills shortages, natural disasters, the weather, too many visitors from head office, expatriates who do not understand the local market and so on. They learnt these excuses from their old colonial masters too.

When the results are excellent then it is totally due to the hard work and expertise of these local bosses.

Tip For Your Trip

Always ingratiate yourself with the local bosses. Never alienate them. The consequences will be dire.

98 INVITATIONS

As mentioned previously, people in unusual countries are much more hospitable than people back home. Even the top people can be hospitable. It will not be often they meet strange people like you and therefore, as a diversion and amusement for their family they will invite you home to their colonial villas in the suburbs.

You should consider this a great honour, even if the servants do the cooking.

On no occasion should you refuse this invitation.

On arrival it is essential that you demonstrate the best manners possible. Here are the best manners possible:

(a) Go well-dressed (even if they say they want you to be comfortable).

(b) Present to your host a bottle of Black Label whisky. This is essential.

(c) Present to your host's wife a piece of exquisite Royal Doulton pottery.

(d) Admire the Mercedes parked in the driveway, along with the Range Rover and the small Nissan his wife drives.

(e) Admire the house, especially the swimming pool and the blooming bougainvillea.

(f) Admire your host's kids.

(g) Admire the paintings on the dining room wall (often these will have been purchased from the railings at Green Park in London).

(h) Admire the wide range of artefacts (elephant tusks, tiger skins etc.) strategically located throughout the house.

(j) Admire the furniture including the wide screen television (which will be kept on throughout the meal).

(k) Admire the dress the host's wife is wearing (she will be overweight).

(l) Say how much you love the food that is being served.

(m) Say how fascinated you have been by the lovely country they live in.

On no occasion should you refuse any food that is offered to you, even if it is completely inedible (and this has happened to me on many occasions). Normally you will be asked to serve yourself from a dish offered by the servant. The secret is to help yourself to an incredibly small portion and then spread it thinly across your plate to make it look large. Then eat it very slowly, thus entitling you to refuse further offers.

Do not talk about politics, religion or other controversial subjects unless your host raises them. Even then do not offer a view but just listen and give the appearance of nodding and agreeing. He will then think he is very wise.

Always follow up the following day with a thank you call saying how much you enjoyed the evening, even if you all talked a load of nonsense and the food was horrid.

Tip For Your Trip

The same as for the section on Stomach Ailments. Take six litres of whisky with you. You can then use these for gifts when invited to dinner parties. Also take with you a good cross-selection of Royal Doulton pottery.

99 HYPOCRISY

Astute readers of this incredibly serious and well-meaning book will have deduced (or is it inferred?) that one of the prime qualities required of any traveller to an unusual country is hypocrisy.

In unusual countries as well as back home hypocrisy is vitally important and surpasses democracy, theocracy, autocracy, bureaucracy, mediocrity and necromancy in the exigencies of its demands. As a fine art hypocrisy rivals diplomacy. The real experts are the aristocracy of any country.

In unusual countries woe betide any person who speaks his (or her) mind and tries to express a genuinely held opinion. Openness, honesty and the truth are all right in principle but in practice are often set aside in the quest for short-term gain, power and influence.

Local advocates of equal opportunities have no place in unusual countries and tend to emigrate so they can wave their flags about discrimination and unfair practices in the countries that have just welcomed them (they rarely speak of the unequal opportunities that exist back home).

Local politicians are sufficiently adept at convincing the world that there is democracy in their countries when there isn't and world politicians are sufficiently adept at turning a blind eye to this when it suits them.

My best advice when visiting an unusual country is to be all things to all men (be careful about being all things to all women). It is essential that you develop the fine art of saying exactly what local people want you to say, nothing will please them more. They will reciprocate and in this way you will have a perfectly harmonious relationship enabling you to call upon each other for a multitude of favours.

The extreme demands of hypocrisy in unusual countries means that you will have to develop your rare talents for flattering people, for agreeing with everyone and for pretending to be what you are not. In unusual countries the mere fact of your visit will lead them to think that you are a very important person in your own country. You should take care not to delude them of this view.

Your standing in the eyes of locals will be diminished rapidly if you make yourself out to be the ordinary, inconsequential tosspot that you really are. You should never tell them the truth, for example, that you have never met the Royal Family and that they have never heard of you.

Tips For Your Trip

You would be well-advised to read Henry Kissinger's book on Diplomacy.

Furthermore you should study in-depth the last four presidents of the USA and Prime Ministers of Great Britain for excellent case studies in hypocrisy.

100 PRAISE

Those of you searching for paradise will not find it in an unusual country. Nor will you find it at home.

You know, and I know, that this little world of ours is far from perfect. The imperfections I have been advising you about in this learned book are not intended as criticism. I actually love these countries. What's more, if you gave me the task (and I might create it) I could write a similar book about Britain and its many imperfections. Writing one about the USA would be even easier.

During the last five years I have visited over twenty different countries, some on a number of occasions. As a result, I have benefited from a wide range of experiences upon which this book is based. Despite all the afflictions I report, and which you need to be prepared for, my main aim in travelling to any unusual country has been to find the good in that country. Invariably the good is to be found in the people I meet albeit not necessarily in what they do.

I find it helps relationships enormously if you can find something genuine to praise in each country and then tell people about it. Here are some examples I have used during recent years:

(a)   I just love your country. I love the climate, the pure air and the people are fantastic.

(b)   I really think this country has great potential. Your people are so dynamic and positive.

(c)   I'm very impressed with all the progress that has been made here since my last visit ten years ago. Things have changed for the better.

(d)   The people in your country are so friendly and helpful. I just love coming here.

It is also in order to praise individuals and compliment them on their smart dress, or their hard work, or their exceptional help.

Conversely, with the exception of one thing, you should never complain to a local about their country. The exception is traffic jams. Everyone is allowed to complain about traffic jams.

If there is any genuine complaining to do leave it to your local friends. Like us; they are very good at moaning and groaning.

Summarily just forget about the nasty things in unusual countries. If they do prey on your mind, take notes and write books about them like I do!

Tip For Your Trip

Take with you a large notebook.

On the left-hand page write down the things you like about the unusual country you are in.

On the right-hand page write down the things you don't like.

When prompted refer to the left-hand page when seeking to praise the country.

CHAPTER 7

STRANGE EXPERIENCES: THINGS TO SEE AND AVOID IN UNUSUAL COUNTRIES

Experiences in unusual countries are a bit like the Turner Prize: strange.

Okay, Tracy Emin's 'My bed' duly unmade did not win the Turner Prize in 1999 but Chris Ofili's painting with elephant dung 'No Woman, No Cry' did in 1998. Another winner was Martin Creed in 2001 with 'The lights going on and off' whilst if we go back to the early 1990s you will find Damien Hirst's dead animals in formaldehyde. Gilbert and George's 'Naked Shit Paintings' (1995) warrent a mention here too.

Your visits to Tate Britain in London to see the Turner Prize shortlist will prepare you exceptionally well for the wide range of strange experiences you will benefit from when visiting unusual countries.

This chapter presents a random sample of such experiences. The key is to approach them with an open mind and, most importantly, to be non-judgemental. I confess to failing on the latter count.

101 POTHOLES

Rifle-touting soldiers are not the main danger on your travels, taxi drivers are. Second in danger to taxi-drivers are potholes. The two go together. The biggest and best potholes are found in unusual countries, often in the pavement along which you are walking. They are a sight to be wondered at. I am surprised more potholes are not shortlisted for the Turner Prize.

None of this namby-pamby stuff we have in the UK about having cones, white and red barriers and little flashing orange lights around the potholes to warn you off and keep you nice and safe. None of this ridiculous stuff about suing the authorities if you fall into a pothole and break your leg. In unusual countries people expect you to have eyes and use common sense.

These potholes are great and really should be seen. Some of them are fifteen feet deep with revolting black liquid, possibly sewage, swirling down below. Some of them have sharp bits of metal jutting out of them. The more boring potholes are merely filled with rubble and masses of litter.

Like most things in life these potholes are there for a purpose. It is to keep drunks off the street. One of the civilised aspects of staying in unusual countries is that you never see drunks swaggering around. If you want to get drunk in an unusual country you do it in private. To do so in public risks falling into a pothole, or, if the secret police are around, being pushed into a pothole. That's the only time these potholes ever get filled. On the death certificate they write 'Disappeared drunk down a pothole'. The insurance companies never pay up for this or any other type of pothole death.

Tip For Your Trip

The best pothole detectors come in the form of a white walking stick. I would take one with you on your trip and use it when out walking. This has the added advantage that in crowds people won't bump into you.

102 UNFINISHED BUILDINGS

Unemployed builders reading this book could do no better than pack up their toolkits and head for an unusual country.

Here you will be guaranteed to find a huge number of unfinished buildings worthy of any piece of modern sculpture. They are everywhere. They normally stand semi-erect with floors suspended around rusting reinforced steel uprights. There might be the occasional outside wall but definitely no windows. With one exception (I'll come on to this later) you will never see anybody working on these unfinished buildings.

I have seen unfinished buildings on mountainsides, in the desert, on streets that go nowhere, along the main roads to airports, in the middle of city centres and most annoyingly next to the hotels I have staying in.

The only unfinished buildings that people ever work on are in fact those next door to hotels I am staying in. The noise for most part of the day is unbearable and the sight even worse.

I think the reason for all these unfinished buildings is that people start constructing them and when they are halfway up they realise they have forgotten to lay on supplies of water, electricity and sewage.

As a word of caution, if you are tempted to work on one of these unfinished building sites normal safety regulations do not apply. You will never be expected to wear safety helmets or take any other precaution that is nowadays taken for granted.

Tip For Your Trip

During your sightseeing in unusual countries should you go looking for unfinished buildings always wear a safety helmet. To be on the safe side take one with you.

103 ROAD SIGNS AND TYRE STUDIES

I often sit in traffic jams studying tyres. It is remarkable but in unusual countries tyres do not have treads. None of this nonsense about a minimum tread of 1.6 mm. Here the tyres on the buses and the trucks are just bald.

I was told by a friendly person on the hotel reception that I should allow half an hour for the journey from the centre of the city to the airport. So I allowed one hour. Well over one hour later we were still stuck in a traffic jam with no airport in sight.

The driver turned left and turned right. He did this many times. I hoped he knew where he was going because I didn't. The streets in this capital have no names and there are no road signs. Back in my part of the world there are friendly direction signs such as 'AIRPORT' straight ahead on them and for those who cannot speak English or cannot read there is a picture of an aeroplane.

In this particular unusual country there is none of that. There are no direction signs. I presume it is because everyone in this country is so well educated that they all know were the airport is and are not stupid enough to require signposts. It has the added advantage that if a rebel army from the north invades the soldiers will not know where the airport is either.

When I sit in these traffic jams I have a wonderful little game. As a boy my father used to take us for rides in traffic jams and we used to play 'I spy'. I have now come up with a more sophisticated adaptation of this game to while away the hours sitting in the backs of taxis and inhaling the black exhaust smoke so prevalent in unusual countries. It is to study the signs on shops and restaurants. Here are some of the more interesting ones I have come across:

Sign outside a restaurant:

You have tried the best, now come here and try the rest

Sign outside a village hall:

Young persons draining hall

Sign above a medical practice:

Specialist in water

Sign outside a car showroom:

All our cars are guaranteed genuine

Sign outside a bakers:

> *Tasty tarts for your enjoyment night and day*

Sign above a supermarket:

> *Floral 3-ply toilet tissue adds beauty to your home*

Sign advertising a local bank:

> *We take your money and keep it*

I almost wish I hadn't arrived at the airport, but there I was, pushing through crowds, filling in countless forms, being quizzed by innumerable officials before discovering my flight had been delayed.

Tip For Your Trip

When visiting unusual countries play this sign-reading game. Take careful notes in that nice big fat exercise book you always carry with you.

104 STREET MARKETS

In unusual countries no town or city is complete without a colourful street market where you can purchase all the things that have been stolen from you and your friends. Also available will be cheap imitations of the latest fashion handbags, Italian shoes and Scottish knitwear. Vast displays of local produce will also be available at unbelievably low prices along with hundreds of carved wooden statues made in China but passed off as local ethnic art.

These markets will be redolent with many classic smells and colours. A nice little touch is often the sewage trickling down the streets that border the markets. If you are a foreigner (which you will be) everyone will stare at you and then will try to entice you to purchase the products on their stalls. Do not be tempted unless you feel really charitable as whatever you purchase will be totally useless. As soon as it rains the dye will come out of that lovely handbag you purchased and your fake shoes will fall apart. The food is sometimes of a quality you would not give to your dog back home.

Most times you will be unable to access these stalls because the thronging crowd is so thick the market becomes impenetrable. This is when you are at highest risk. As you gaze lovingly at the picturesque sights and try to take photos with that expensive digital camera of yours you will be jostled into the heaving swirl of people and deftly relieved of all your valuables. Pick-pocketing is a highly honed craft in unusual countries. You can put your losses down to experience. It is no good reporting the theft to the police in order to claim against your travel insurance. The police will be in league with the thieves and merely shrug their shoulders. These are the sort of foolish things foreign tourists do.

The amazing thing about these street markets is that many of the stallholders speak English. It is a lesson they have all learnt: If you want to earn good money in this world you need to speak English.

Tip For Your Trip

Never take a lot of money or anything of value to a street market. As soon as you enter one as a foreigner you are expected to spend money, and if you don't you will be deprived of it by some other method.

105 SHOPS

To impress professionals on your travels you need to start talking about micro finance. It's what they have in unusual countries. When you go into a local shop you will find it difficult to buy a large pack of anything. As they say small is beautiful. Shops in unusual countries sell things in a small way.

On one occasion I was in a pharmacy browsing the different coloured condoms by the counter when the beggar I'd just given twenty cents to outside came up and purchased one sleeping tablet with the two coins I'd just given him.

Afterwards, thinking I was in the queue, the beautiful assistant diverted my attention from the condoms and asked if she could help. Instinctively I asked for aspirin. She pulled out some scissors on a string and cut off one aspirin from a foil pack. She charged me twenty cents. In attempting to make conversation she told me that most customers only purchased one or two tablets at a time. That's all they could afford. If they were on a course of antibiotics they would come in each day to purchase one pill.

At the grocery store nearby I noticed that it was possible to buy one tea bag at a time or one sachet of shampoo. Elsewhere you can buy an individual cigarette or tomato.

In unusual countries most people do not buy in bulk but purchase one little thing at a time; just enough for the day because that's all the money they have in the world. Manufacturers have discovered this and now produce micro-sized portions of virtually every commodity. You can even purchase a 50 ml carton of milk.

Expressed another way: it is only the very rich people who go to the supermarket to buy a 12-pack of toilet rolls. Most ordinary folks don't use toilet paper. A ten cent newspaper can go a long way.

Tip For Your Trip

Keep your coins and spend them on the little things.
If you prefer to be generous give them to beggars.

106 MUSIC AND DANCE

Now I will reveal the mystery of life. The reason people in unusual countries are so happy is that they really know how to make music and dance. This is something you can never take home with you. When you buy a CD of the music it never sounds the same at home and you will lose at least 90% of the original joy.

However, in an unusual country you will revel in the beauty and art of exquisite music and dance which you invariably come across when you least expect it. All the minor deficiencies I have so lovingly detailed in the previous sections of this book pale into infinitesimal insignificance compared with the emotionally energising and positively uplifting spirits you will experience when your heart synchronises with rhythms of the night.

To see bright-eyed children dancing out of school, to find a lone man squatting in the street lovingly strumming a guitar, to hear the hypnotic rhythms of distant drums is enough to move anyone towards a total re-evaluation of life and the world we live in.

It is not money that makes people rich but the music they create for others to enjoy along with other art forms. At home we have made life a science. In unusual countries it is still an art. Happiness comes from the heart, not the mind. Science is a function of the mind whilst art is a function of the heart wherein rests the soul. In unusual countries you can discover people with heart and soul, people without the financial riches that so-called scientific progress brings.

Perhaps I am perverse but give me the choice between a city with clinical efficiency and sanitised surfaces, and a city with the colour of squalor and eccentric creativity, I would always choose the latter. With globalisation too many cities across the world are becoming too well ordered, too similar and too boring. They are being constructed according to the financial prescriptions of billionaire capitalists.

The end result is that all around the world cities are having their hearts and souls ripped out and replaced with the constructs of complex computerised design.

Give me the eccentricities of people's hearts and the irregular social arrhythmia you find in unusual countries. From these will spring the harmonies of the soul and the real rhythm of life.

Tip For Your Trip

Never approach an unusual country in a rational frame of mind. Bare your heart and soul, as the locals do, and you will love every minute. Well almost!

107 OPERA

When it comes to wondrous music and dance in unusual countries there is one exception. Opera.

Every capital city of every unusual country stages at least one opera per year. This will always coincide with your visit and there will always be somebody to invite you along. You must go for the experience.

The opera house itself will be an incredibly magnificent modern building that is incredibly badly run. In fact, along with the government palace it will be the only magnificent building in the city. A previous president will have had it built with foreign funds and had it named after him.

Only important people in unusual countries go to the opera and they only go for one reason. That is to be seen there. They do not go to listen to the opera which is purely incidental. To be seen there you can do one of two things:

(a) Arrive early in your fur coat, top hat and gold jewellery and make sure you recognise and greet anyone of note. It is quite in order to ignore people who are not important unless you wish to appear patronising.

(b) Arrive very late, just as the curtain is rising and make sure you make an entrance as dramatic as the diva who is about to appear on the stage. (Opera houses in unusual countries still have curtains). People who do this normally have seats right in the middle of the front row.

When the opera is finished people will exchange superficial opinions about it and your host undoubtedly will ask yours. You can rehearse your opinion in advance, without even having attended the opera. The following lines are useful:

(i)   It is an amazing coincidence but this is my favourite opera.

(ii) I thought the performance was as good as you will get at Covent Garden, the New York Met or La Scala in Milan.

(iii) I thought the tenor/soprano was absolutely wonderful. He/she reminded me of Pavarotti/Callas.

This is all you need to say because nobody will be listening to you.

It is useful to have an opera guide in your hotel bedroom so that you can read a paragraph or two about the opera before attending and therefore conjure up an opinion which has a hint of expertise about it.

Tip For Your Trip

It is wise to take with you a guide to the major operas.

108 RED-LIGHT DISTRICTS

I would hate readers to think that unusual countries are incredibly unsafe places full of hidden dangers such as rats and crazy driving. In fact if you have a tendency towards paranoia and crave safety and security yet still wish to visit an unusual country, then you might wish to stay in one specific area every city has which is incredibly safe and crime-free. This is an area where you are unlikely to be robbed at gunpoint or violently assaulted by soccer hooligans.

These sanctuaries are called red light districts and they are totally dedicated to your entertainment and personal pleasure, comprising as they do many nightclubs, restaurants, cafés, bars and massage parlours (but not brothels - see next section). The last thing owners of these establishments want is problems with criminals as this would drive away rich customers (like you).

So these owners (let's call them the mafia) ensure there is no crime. They even pay a service charge (or informal tax or bribe if you prefer to call it that) to the local police to ensure there are no problems from their side either. The only hassle you are going to get on the streets of red-light districts is from hawkers trying to sell you fake Viagra and stolen sunglasses (so you can't see what's going on).

The advantage of red-light districts is that they are very colourful. For a start, they actually do have red lights (and orange ones too along with flashing yellow, strobing blue and alluring green). They are also full of attractive young people trying to catch your eye and chat you up. If you are very old, fat and ugly like me this can be quite flattering.

Taking my own advice, I normally stay in hotels in the centre of red-light districts. On one occasion after dinner I was sipping coffee in the hotel lounge which had a large window looking out onto the narrow street which was the spine of this red-light district. The other side of the window was a low wall upon which were sitting ten attractive young prostitutes. They were eyeing the passers-by for custom. The most beautiful one of all turned around, saw me sitting in the hotel lounge and then smiled and waved at me. She gesticulated with her hands inviting me for a shoulder massage. To be honest, she was the type of young woman I could fall in love with and divorce even more wives for.

However, my companion who was sipping coffee with me (I was being chaperoned by another beautiful young lady) smiled and informed me that this young prostitute was in fact not a woman at all! My chaperone had noticed that this sexy young prostitute, dressed in sexy female clothing had an Adam's apple. She was what is known as a lady-boy. So in these countries as in our own, there are all types. for all types.

Tip For Your Trip

Always stay in red-light districts.

Always have a chaperone to advise you on matters relating to Adam's apples.

(And if you insist, use condoms).

109 BROTHELS

Most visitors to unusual countries would not know what a brothel looks like. It is not as if you can search in Yellow Pages to find out, or walk through the red-light district to locate signs such as 'Mandy's Brothel, Half price between 5:00 pm to 7:00 pm', or 'Susie's Luxury Brothel', voted the best in a survey of 10,000 business people by the Institute of Brothels.

The aficionados (mainly taxi drivers or hotel concierges) tell me that you have to be careful to differentiate a brothel from:

*   A massage parlour
*   A nightclub
*   A KTV bar (karaoke bar)
*   A lap dancing club
*   The bar in your hotel

There are countries where prostitutes sit in windows and advertise their wares. In unusual countries this sort of exhibitionism is frowned upon. They exercise a much higher degree of discretion.

The experts tell me that in unusual countries brothels tend to be situated in private houses in the suburbs where the rents are lower and the owners can provide bigger bedrooms for the enjoyment of their clients. The best brothels will send a limousine to your hotel to collect and drive you to the establishment. From the outside it will look like a normal colonial house in a rich part of town.

The door will be opened by an attractive young lady who will guide you to a lounge and take payment in advance. Then a succession of beautiful young girls will parade before you with such interesting words as "I am Jade and I am twenty-two" or "I am Candy and I am twenty-three". You then make your choice as if you were selecting Miss World. In some establishments these young women parade topless whilst in others they do not. At least this is what the taxi drivers tell me. They also tell me that if you wish to take the young woman back to your hotel for an in-depth interview about their work (they are officially called sex workers) then the charge will be double.

So there you have it. There is no point in denying what happens in most unusual countries let alone the UK where the legal maximum is two women per brothel.

Tip For Your Trip

Take with you a list of all the brothels in the unusual country (so that you can studiously avoid them). You can print this list off from the internet or alternatively consult the local tourist authority. If your spouse finds this list on you and politely enquires why you are taking it abroad, please show her this page of the book.

110 SLUMS

According to the 2003 UN-Habitat report 'The Challenge of Slums' one third of the world's urban population lives in a slum. That's one billion people. Most of these slums are in unusual countries. I have visited quite a few in my time. I like to undertake what I call reality checks. They peg me back to reality.

On the last occasion I was taken by a priest (he called himself a missionary) to a slum where approximately a million people lived, most of them unemployed. On the other side of the city was an even bigger, and more famous, slum with over three million people.

I saw things that I expected to see and things which I did not expect to see. I expected to see wobbly wooden shacks with corrugated iron roofs, sagging electricity lines, ragged children chasing skinny chickens, sewage trickling down the middle of the muddy path and people queuing with buckets for standpipe water.

Of course I didn't see any violence nor did I see anybody being robbed.

What I didn't expect to see was the millionaires' houses in the middle of the slum. These were magnificent white villas surrounded by tall white walls within which Alsatian dogs barked and shining Mercedes limousines were parked. I am told you get this in most large slums around the world.

What I didn't expect to see were all these happy people. The children were smiling. Their mothers were smiling. Even the men drinking beer at the local drinking houses seemed happy. Many of them were happy to chat to me too. I was even invited into their one-room homes where families of seven might sleep. I kept on saying to myself that with all this poverty and squalor surely they must be unhappy. But they didn't seem to be. Perhaps I have got it wrong.

The paradox is that back home in my country where we have fewer slums and we are all generally better off, there are many people going bonkers with stress related diseases you never seem to find in unusual countries. I struggle with this all the time. It's perhaps why I travel so much. I am trying to fathom out one of the unfathomable mysteries of life. Correct me if I am wrong, but can you really be happy living in a slum? Correct me if I am right, but can you really be happy sitting in that daily traffic jam, working even longer hours and being subjected to an ever increasing intensity of competitive pressures?

A few years ago an intellectual who lived in one of these slums told me "We don't have green parks around here except in people's minds."

Tip For Your Trip

Next time you visit an unusual country take time out to look around a slum. I call it taking a reality check.

111 ARMED HIJACKING

This can be quite serious and occasionally life threatening. To be honest you never know when it is going to happen. It could happen anywhere and any time of the day in an unusual country. It could also happen to anyone, even you!

Before travelling to an unusual country it would be wise to attend a three week training course on what to do in the event of an armed hijacking. Should this not be possible practice with your kids on the stairs, using pretend guns.

The key rules to assimilate and digest when you are hijacked are these:

(a)   Never say "No" when the armed hijacker asks you for something.

(b)   Never argue with an armed hijacker.

(c)   Be polite and courteous at all times.

(d)   Keep calm (i.e. don't scream, become hysterical, cry, look upset or panic).

(e)   Be complimentary (e.g. I am impressed by the calibre of your gun, I really do like these fashionable designer models).

(f)   Do not ask for a receipt for the money and valuables the armed hijacker takes from you.

(g)   Do not ask the armed hijacker to pose for photos.

(h)   Do not report the hijacking to the police (armed hijackers are probably off duty policemen anyway).

You will need to check with your travel insurer to learn if you can claim for ransoms paid out. Don't worry if you are a business traveller as you will probably find that hijacking costs are tax-deductible against expenses. However, the absence of receipts might make things more difficult as bureaucrats normally insist upon them.

Tip For Your Trip

Before visiting an unusual country attend a three week training course on dealing with armed hijacking. Take the handouts with you to refresh your memory whilst in the unusual country.

112 MUGGING

Whilst armed hijacking is relatively rare in an unusual country (say a 1:10 chance) the probability of being mugged is much higher. So be prepared to be mugged, even veterans get mugged.

There are some simple rules you can learn to minimise the consequences of mugging.

Firstly only carry on you an amount of money you will feel comfortable in losing, say between ten and fifty dollars. (The muggers will take offence if you don't have dollars and offer local currency). It is sensible to carry these dollars in low denomination notes to give the impression you are carrying a lot of money.

Have this cash readily available in the top right-hand pocket of your shirt. Do not hesitate to give it to the mugger when prompted.

The more sophisticated mugger will also ask you for your credit card. However, if you study these muggers carefully you will see that they never look at which credit card you are giving them.

Therefore also have available in your top right-hand pocket any old card, but not your real one. I find a Tesco Clubcard quite helpful for this purpose. It is quite useless to a mugger unless he wants to cash in the points at my local Tesco. A Shell V-Power fuel card can also be quite impressive. Every time the mugger uses it you will be clocking up a bundle of Smart Points.

Tip For Your Trip

Always carry a Tesco Clubcard (or equivalent) with you on your visits to unusual countries.

113 KIDNAPPING

During the 1980s kidnapping was prevalent in many unusual countries. However, thanks to books like this it is much less so now. The danger is of course that we all become complacent. Isolated cases of kidnapping are still reported in the press and there are many more which are not. It is therefore sensible to be wise before the event. The following is a short guide to the precautions you should take to minimise the risk of being kidnapped:

(a) Always ensure you are driven around in a small Nissan car.

(b) Never walk alone outside your hotel. Use your best friend as a bodyguard.

(c) Keep away from dangerous areas where kidnappers are likely to lurk.

(d) Never wear your best outfit when out and about.

(e) Wear dirty old jeans and a dirty T-shirt at all times.

(f) If you are a man do not shave on the day you might be kidnapped.

(g) Leave your gold, jewellery and valuables in the security box in your hotel (or preferably at home).

(h) Don't talk to strangers (who might be in league with the kidnappers).

(i) Only tell your closest confidantes of your future whereabouts.

(j) Keep your head down at all times.

(k) Leave false trails.

(l) Walk fast but do not run.

It is also wise to have a contingency plan in the event that these precautions do not work and you are actually kidnapped. Before departing for an unusual country ensure that you:

(i) Appoint a kidnap liaison officer to negotiate on your behalf and represent your interests when your plight receives worldwide publicity. Ideally, this kidnap liaison officer (who could be a member of your family, a friend or someone from work) should be thoroughly trained in kidnap release.

(ii) Agree in advance what your price (ransom) should be for release. The general rule of thumb is as follows: (Your salary x 10) + (your mortgage x 3). Your spouses salary is not normally taken into account unless he or she is kidnapped alongside you. You should also bear in mind that ransoms are not normally tax-deductible. However, kidnappers will normally inflate the ransom demand to allow for tax payments in their home country. The exception is when there is a political motive for the kidnapping, in which case different rules will apply to the formula used for calculation.

(iii) Have printed a kidnap crisis card which you should carry with you at all times when visiting an unusual country. You should hand it to the kidnappers on being kidnapped. This advises them what to do next. Here is an example:

KIDNAP CARD

Dear Kidnapper,

I would politely request that you ring my kidnap liaison officer to negotiate my release. His name is:

John Smith

and he can be contacted 24 hours a day on:

0044 1122 1234 43210 (please reverse charges)

You should ensure that the other side of this card is printed in the local language of the country you are visiting. Not all kidnappers can speak English. If the card can include a mini-photo of you this will prove helpful to the kidnappers and will be appreciated by them. You could even offer to autograph it.

Tip For Your Trip

Have prepared a kidnap crisis card and keep it with you at all times.

More seriously, register your presence in town with the local British Embassy.

114 PRISONS

I have never been to prison in the UK let alone in an unusual country. But I know someone from an unusual country who has.

He tells me that prisons in my country are like five star hotels compared with prisons in most unusual countries. There they do not have proper beds, televisions, home cooking or decent hospitals to recover in when prisoners feel ill.

He told me that if you want to get an idea of what prisons are like in unusual countries you should go and see films such as The Mask of Zorro or Robin Hood: Prince of Thieves. I did, and now I've got the idea: positively medieval.

Prisons in unusual countries are really dangerous places, not only because they are full of dangerous criminals but because the prison staff are even worse. It amazes me how they get these criminals into prison in the first place because most police forces in these countries are both incompetent and corrupt. Surely, if you have stolen a lot of money the least you could do is bribe the police officer who arrests you not to send you to prison?

Mercifully, most foreign visitors to unusual countries who commit crimes and get captured do not get sent to prison, unless they are involved with the drug trade, commit ghastly murders, perpetrate perverse sex practices or offend the regime. If you just commit an ordinary crime you get sent home with a warning.

Most of us are, of course, not criminals and would not dream of committing a crime. However, there is behaviour we take as ordinary in our country that's considered to be criminal in some unusual countries because it offends the regime. Such behaviour includes complaining about the government, taking photographs of military establishments (two rusting tanks), lying naked on a beach, practising your own religion or getting drunk. Once you are in prison for offences against the regime the truth will never come out because the authorities will invent it for you. The wheels of judicial bureaucracy will take years to turn (so many officials waiting for a bribe) and you will while away your time watching other prisoners murder each other and waste away with all manner of hideous afflictions.

It is therefore best to swot up on the restrictions that apply when you visit any unusual country. In this way you can modify your own behaviour and avoid being sent to prison.

Tip For Your Trip

An authoritative guide to the laws and restrictions that apply to people visiting unusual countries.

115 WAR ZONES

Most unusual countries have war zones in the north. Due to religious, tribal, economic or political differences there is always a minority of people in these countries who think they would be better off running their own show.

To achieve this they go around massacring people who do not speak the same language as them, or who dress differently, or who pray differently or who even look differently. These people then retaliate by going around massacring the people who tried to massacre them.

This is all an attempt to make the world a better place to live.

These massacres are often supported by Western nations who have many vested interests, for example, a viable arms industry, the exploitation of valuable resources in these zones and the need to put their man in charge of this unusual country. Such wars and massacres also divert attention away from political problems back home. As far as Western nations are concerned, democracy and principles are irrelevant and are only insisted upon if they anticipate it will secure them the result they want.

When you are visiting an unusual country it is wise to avoid these war zones unless you are a reporter and want to make a name for yourself by being kidnapped or killed.

Normally, war zones are miles away from the capital city where life goes on quite normally and the squalor sits quite comfortably with the rich people you will see and meet in the hotel.

It is advisable not to mention the war to your local friends unless they raise the subject first. Never ever take sides except to subtly hint that you are taking the side of the person speaking. However you should never ever directly assert an opinion as this might land you in gaol. (There are spies everywhere when there are wars in the north).

Tip For Your Trip

Before travelling, obtain the latest intelligence report about the war zones in the country you are visiting. This will bring you bang up to date with all the latest massacres.

116 PEOPLE STANDING AROUND

One feature I have noticed in many unusual countries is that there are a large number of people standing around doing nothing.

One day in an unusual country I was working in my hotel room tapping away on my laptop. As I began to suffer from repetitive strain injury I got up to stretch my legs and stare out of the third floor window. Across the road I noticed a man in a blue shirt and black trousers standing there. That was all he was doing. He was not talking to anyone. He was not selling anything. He didn't seem to be going anywhere. I thought nothing of it, in fact I did think a little bit about it. I thought he was waiting for a friend to give him a lift.

I returned to my laptop and forgot about this man. Somehow I got into flow with my writing project and the words started pouring out. I just couldn't stop. Three hours later I relieved myself of the pain that was now afflicting various parts of my body.

I looked out of the window again and there was this man still standing there. I was tempted to go and invite him for an in-depth interview. But then I realised that I had observed thousands of people in unusual countries standing around doing nothing. Often they sit around and do nothing. The really poor people lie on the pavements and do nothing.

Perhaps it is a good thing to do nothing. You can't get into trouble that way. You eat less. You have more time to think. And most of all it means you can avoid arguing with people back home who are doing all the things you don't like.

Tip For Your Trip

Practice doing nothing for a change, especially when visiting an unusual country. It will be a novel experience.

CHAPTER 8

IN PREPARATION FOR TRAVEL TO UNUSUAL COUNTRIES: THE FINAL LISTS

Careful studying of the previous seven chapters will have been the equivalent of a fun-packed three year university degree course in 'Travel to Unusual Countries'. The benefits to any reader will be enormous.

Now is the time to summarily reflect on the various facets of such travel and we will do this by way of four exceptionally useful check-lists.

117 CHECKLIST A:

50 Things Difficult To Find In Unusual Countries

1   Fresh dairy butter, fresh milk and real cream
2   Cheddar cheese
3   A pork pie
4   Decent bacon
5   A good breakfast
6   Bacteria free burgers
7   Pickle and pickled onions
8   Home baked apple pie
9   Any type of fruit which isn't bruised, dirty or rotting
10 A nice cup of tea
11 Aromatic coffee
12 Fresh doughnuts
13 Clean tap water
14 Health foods
15 Drinkable wine
16 Trouser presses
17 A wide variety or choice of anything
18 Things that work for more than five minutes
19 People that work for more than five minutes
20 Hassle free airports
21 Good customer service
22 Cuddly cats
23 Safe sex
24 Any public toilets
25 Clean toilets
26 Roads without potholes
27 Safe drivers
28 Reliable taxis
29 Cars without dents
30 Car parks
31 Public transport you want to use
32 Anything you want to use

33   Today's newspapers
34   Interesting TV programmes
35   The latest films
36   The latest chart music
37   Honest politicians
38   Honest policemen
39   Clean beaches
40   Well-maintained parks
41   Well run museums
42   Great shops
43   A bookshop with a book you want
44   A copy of this book
45   The genuine article
46   Punctuality
47   Clinical efficiency
48   Competence in dealing with emergencies
49   Sanitised surfaces
50   Perfection

118 CHECKLIST B:

What You Can Buy With 50 Dollars

Fifty dollars comes in quite handy in unusual countries. In fact, most things in unusual countries can be bought for less than fifty dollars. Here are just a few examples:

A chauffeur driven car for a day

Five nights in a 3* hotel (including breakfast)

One night in a 4* hotel (including dinner and breakfast)

Four hours in a 5* hotel (excluding partner)

A luxury meal for four (excluding drinks)

A bottle of imported whisky

Two bottles of imported wine

Three hours in a casino

A good woman for a night

A bad woman for a night

A good woman for a week (to cook, clean and care for your kids)

A four hour massage

Four one-hour massages

A one hour massage with four masseuses

An ancient relic (either stolen from an archaeological investigation at a nearby historic site or a fake)

An original oil painting by a local artist

A large wooden sculpture

A pair of new shoes and a new outfit

Two made-to-measure shirts or blouses

A one-way ticket on a domestic airline

Half the insurance for a one-way ticket on a domestic airline

A visa to a neighbouring country

A ticket to the opera (held once a year)

A decent bribe

A trip on a tour bus for two

A personal security guard for a week

A visit to a doctor

A five minute operation in a public hospital

500 coins to give to beggars

119 CHECKLIST C:

Last Minute Supplies For Travelling Around Unusual Countries

After this page is Checklist D which summarises all the tips in this book and lists all those things you need to pack for your trip to smooth your way through an unusual country and to address all the problems which you are sure to experience.

There will be additional items you forget and which will be unavailable as soon as you are out of the hotel exploring the unusual terrain.

Mercifully, most of these last minute supplies are available free of charge from your airline or your hotel. What I normally do is carry a large carrier bag around with me and when nobody is looking I plop the required item into it.

Here is a suggested list of last minute essential supplies, although you might wish to amend it to meet your own specific requirements.

Bags of peanuts (available on your flight)

Small bottles of wine (available on your flight)

Small miniatures of liqueurs (available on your flight)

Small packs of biscuits/cookies (available on your flight)

Dry meat (available in your hotel)

Napkins. These can double as toilet tissue.(available in your hotel).

Small knives, forks and spoons (available on your flight)

Sachets of salt, pepper and sugar (available in restaurants)

Wet tissues (available on your flight)

Toothpicks (available in restaurants)

Cans of mineral water, juices and colas (available on your flight but check the use-by date)

Fresh fruit (available at breakfast in your -hotel but wash first)

Bread rolls and pastries (available at breakfast in your hotel)

Tea bags, sachets of coffee and milk powder (available in your hotel)

Pens, paper and magazines (available on your flight & in your hotel room)

Playing cards (available on old aircraft only)

Washbags (available when you chat up the flight attendants serving business class)

Hair-dryer (available in your hotel) Very useful when climbing mountains or on the beach after skinny-dipping in the sea

Shampoo, bath foam and lotions (available in your hotel room and when you chat up the housekeeping staff)

Soap (available on your flight and in your hotel room)

Toilet rolls (available on your flight but not always in your hotel room)

Large knives, forks and spoons (available in your hotel's restaurant)

Slippers and bathrobe (available in some hotel rooms)

Face flannels and towels (available in some hotel rooms)

Sweets (available on your flight or in hotel conference rooms just wander in when no one is looking and pinch a handful)

You will see from the above that the experienced traveller to an unusual country never goes wanting and never has to pay for last minute emergency supplies.

Furthermore, these small items make excellent gifts to beggars and your friends if you are too mean to purchase gifts.

120 CHECKLIST D:

Things To Pack In Preparation For A Visit To An Unusual Country

(This is extracted from the tips in the previous seven chapters)

It is essential that you pack the following items for each visit to an unusual country. (As indicated in brackets below there are a few items which might be available locally)

A small portable television

A strong standard size cardboard box

A ladies high heel shoe

Six Cuban cigars

A fresh juicy onion (can be purchased locally if available)

An old fashioned headmaster's cane

A pair of cheap chopsticks

Dirty and stinking clothes (these can be accumulated en route)

A lifelike facemask

Some best fillet steak (can be purchased locally if available)

A stray cat (easy enough to acquire locally)

Armour-plated metal waistcoast

Jockstrap

Gorilla-proof sunglasses

A baseball bat

A polystyrene cape

A wide brimmed black hat

A plastic sheet designed for incontinent people

Three specimen bottles

A copy of Edward Wilson's book *The Diversity of Life*

Two wet sponges

A sick bag

Lots of shiny pens with your name on

Water purifying tablets

A carrier bag containing six half-litre cartons of long-life milk

Three litres of mineral water

A copy of a recipe for a club sandwich

Noseplugs

Plenty of perfume

An extra pair of trousers

Two extra pairs of underwear

Three damp J Cloths

Six rolls of fluffy toilet paper

A stomach pump

Ten duty-free packs of cigarettes

Six litres of whisky

Your yellow health passport

Sixty strawberry flavoured ribbed condoms

A contingency plan (in case of accident)

A first aid kit: (containing all the items listed in Section 35: Medical Supplies)

A confirmation letter that you have a private air ambulance standing-by

A breathing mask

A laminated photocopy of Section 45 relating to Dying

A bucket

A small pocket torch

A candle, a candlestick and a box of matches

A graph book, a black and a red pen, and a ruler

Three alarm clocks

Two hundred dollars to give away

A Corby Trouser Press

A multi-adaptor plug

Two large boxes of detergent

One large bottle of fabric conditioner

Ten plastic coat-hangers

A long chain

Six assorted pairs of shoelaces

Any book which is better than a television programme. In other words, any book

A toolkit comprising: (i) Swiss army penknife (ii) a hammer (iii) a long screwdriver (iv) a pack of fuses (v) a variety of fuse wires (vi) ordinary wire (vii) some string and a good selection of screws and cable clips (viii) a pacemaker battery

A stopwatch

Lots of scrap paper

A heavy pair of sandals

A nice thick woolly cardigan

Sleeping pills

Telephone numbers for everyone

A urine bottle and stopper

A fast driver phrase book

A long luggage strap

A card with the address of your hotel printed in the local language

A detailed map of how to get to your hotel

The railway timetable for the country you are visiting

A can of warm cola (normally available locally)

Your cellphone (kept switched-on at all times)

A large notebook

The *Complete Works of Shakespeare*

A compass

A further one hundred, twenty dollar bills

Assorted stickers including one "Remember to get out of the way of drivers flashing headlights"

Your UK driving licence

The latest book on positive thinking

A further two hundred single dollar notes

Four open first class return air tickets to anywhere

Two watches, one for each hand

A large purse

A huge collection of coins (collectible in an unusual country)

A manual and DVD on negotiating skills

100 personalised name cards (any name will do)

Six pieces of exquisite Royal Doulton pottery

Henry Kissingers book *Diplomacy*

A guide to international etiquette

A white walking stick

A safety helmet

A guide to the major operas

A list of all brothels in the country (printed from the internet)

The handouts from a three week training course on dealing with armed hijacking

A Tesco Clubcard (or equivalent)

A kidnap crisis card

An authoritative guide to the laws and restrictions to visitors in the country

The latest intelligence report about war zones in the country

A valid visa for the country

Your passport

Other books by David Freemantle

The Biz

50 Things That Make A Great Difference To Team Motivation and Leadership

The Buzz

50 Little Things That Make A Great Difference To World Class Customer Service

How To Choose

The Eight Suns of Asian Service

The Stimulus Factor

What Customers Like About You

100 Days In The Life of a Superboss

Profitboss

Other titles from Zymurgy Publishing

Zymurgy titles can be ordered from all good bookshops. Alternatively you may contact Zymurgy Publishing by telephone at 0191 276 2425 or e-mail info@zymurgypublishing.com or snail mail, Zymurgy Publishing, Hoults Estate, Walker Road, Newcastle upon Tyne NE6 2HL

Natural North
by Allan Potts
Foreword by the Duke of Northumberland
A photographic celebration of flora and fauna in the North of England. Supporting text provides background information. Sections cover; high fells, upland, woodland, agricultural, coastal and urban areas.
ISBN 1 903506 00X hb 160pp £16.99

Bent Not Broken
by Lauren Roche
Lauren Roche's autobiography; an abused child, stowaway, stripper, prostitute, drug abuser. She turned her life around to become a doctor. An international best seller. Lauren has been interviewed by Lorraine Kelly, Esther Rantzen, Johnny Walker, Simon Mayo and others.
ISBN 1 903506 026 pb 272pp + 8pp plate section £6.99

Life On The Line
by Lauren Roche
Following on from Bent Not Broken the book covers Lauren's life once she becomes a doctor. Bankruptcy, depression, a suicide attempt - and the shock revelation that her son was a sex offender. What can a mother do when she suspects that one of her children is being abused? What happens when you discover that the abused child has become an abuser?
ISBN 1 903506 050 pb 192pp + 8pp plate section £6.99

A Lang Way To The Pawnshop

by Thomas Callaghan

Introduction by Sid Chaplin

An autobiographical account of growing up in 1930s urban Britain; a family of ten, two bedrooms, no wage earner. An amusing insight into a period of history still in living memory. Originally published in the 1970s, the title is a Geordie classic.

ISBN 1 903506 018 pb 144pp £6.99

The Krays: The Geordie Connection

by Steve Wraith and Stuart Wheatman

Foreword by Dave Courtney

After seeing the Krays at a funeral on the news (aged ten) Steve writes letters, meets the brothers and eventually becomes one of 'the chaps'. The book is about the Krays final years and how they ran things on the outside.

ISBN 1 903506 042 pb 240pp + 8pp plate section£6.99

The River Tyne From Sea to Source

by Ron Thornton

Foreword by Robson Green

A collection of nearly eighty water colours and hundreds of pencil drawings following the River Tyne from outside the harbour to the source of the North and South Tyne rivers. Supporting text provides a wealth of information on the history surrounding the Tyne.

ISBN 1 903506 034 hb 160pp £16.99

A Memoir of The Spanish Civil War

by George Wheeler

Foreword by Jack Jones

Edited by David Leach

Thousands from across the world went to Spain to form the International Brigades; many did not return. Through George Wheeler's experience and memories of the Spanish Civil War you will discover what the war was really like. What were they fighing for? Why did the Spanish people fail in their fight against facism? Dramatised for the BBC Worldservice.

1 903506 077 pb 192pp + 8pp plate section £8.99

Alcatraz Island Memoirs of a Rock Doc

by Milton Daniel Beacher, M.D

Edited by Dianne Beacher Perfit

Milton Daniel Beacher, M.D. arrived on Alcatraz Island a naive and compassionate young doctor. One year later he left with a journal. It chronicled the suicides, discipline problems, force feedings , and details of a long strike and successful escape.

He also penned conversations with famous prisoners like Al Capone, Alvin Karpis and Machine Gun Kelly. Dr Beacher later worve the journal into a vivid acoount of life on the Rock.

1 903506 085 pb 240 pp + 8pp plate section £6.99

Back Lanes and Muddy Pitches

by Robert Rowell

A book about football and growing up. Robert Rowell's football career starts within earshot and eyesight of mum; with lamp posts for floodlights and garage doors for goals. Neighbours are relieved when their local footballers are old enough to cross the main road; matches in the park with jumpers for goal posts. Robert gets the utlimate call-up, a place in the school team. When he starts work, he discovers the joys of Sunday league football.

An entertaining celebration of a lifetime playing football.

1 903506 123 pb 288 pp £6.99

Soapy Business

by John Solomon

Set in the late 1950s and early 1960s in the days before supermarkets and identikit town centres. Shops were family owned by eccentrics with 'idiosyncratic retail management style'. John Solomon reveals the cut and thrust world of the soapy salesman - with ongoing tussles with grocers and devious methods of beating his competitors. 'Suds Law' If things could go wrong, they often did.

A burgeoning career and a highly desirable company car created many opportunities for an eager, single young man coming-of-age.

A charming and lighthearted read, full of warmth and optimism.

1 903506 14X pb 192 pp £7.99

Wili Whizkas Tall Tales and Lost Lives
by Paws and Claws

Willi Whizkas is an ordinary cat who shares his home with two humans. He is fed up with the same old cat food everyday, envious of his friends - they all have cat flaps and he hates the vet.

His life is far from humdrum and routine. Willi Whizkas has a great group of friends, loves exploring and haveing adventures.

Willi Whizkas is a naughty but lovable cat.

Purrfect reading for all cat lovers.

1 903506 18 2 pb 256 pp £7.99

Northstars
by Chris Phipps, Sid Smith and John Tobler

A celebration of musicians with North-Eastern roots, *Northstars* is based on exclusive interviews from Royal Television Society award winning Tyne Tees series of the same name. The book honours the role of North-East musicians in the history of popular music.

Eric Burdon, Eliza Carthy, David Coverdale, Dubstar, Bryan Ferry, Brian Johnson, Mark Knopfler, Lindisfarne, Jez Lowe, Hank Marvin, Paddy McAloon, John Miles, Pauline Murray, PJ & Duncan, John Steel, Dave Stewart, Sting, Neil Tennant, Bruce Welch and others.

1 903506 093 pb 256 pp £12.99

The Pennine Way
by Tony Hopkins

The Pennine Way was opened officially in 1965 when it became Britain's first national trail. It starts in Derbyshire's Peak District, passes through the north of England and ends just over the Scottish border at Kirk Yetholm. It is considered to be Britain's greatest footpath.

Tony Hopkins is the writer of the official guides to the Pennine Way. In this book he celebrates the natural beauty of the path through photography, illustrations and a narrative that provides a fascinating background.

1 903506131 hb 160 pp colour photographs throughout £16.99

The Little Book On How To Be A Lady

A book that addresses many of the issues and predicaments that modern women face on a daily basis. How to compare men to shoes, choose a man by the soup that he chooses, cope with 2 blokes fighting over you, walk past building sites, textually flirt, meet the parents and be ready for anything animal, vegtable or genital.

It is essential reading for all modern women.

1903506 190 pb 128pp £2.99

The Little Book of What Men Don't Understand About Women

Since the beginning of time men have struggled to understand women. Their behaviour, attitudes, shopping, clothing, moods swings and general domestic arrangements. This book explores feminine mysteries and provides concise explanations - that men may be able to comprehend. Why do they go to the toilet in pairs, have so many pairs of shoes and so on?

1903506 220 pb 128pp £2.99